In Who

Finding your God-given identity at work

Andy Black

O&U
Onwards & Upwards

Onwards and Upwards Publishers

4 The Old Smithy, London Road, Rockbeare,
EX5 2EA, United Kingdom.

www.onwardsandupwards.org

First edition, published in the United Kingdom by Onwards and Upwards Publishers (2023).

ISBN: 978-1-78815-941-8
Typeface: Sabon LT

Endorsements

Every believer has prayed, 'Your kingdom come, Your will be done, on earth as it is in heaven.' This excellent book by Andy Black will baptise you into the kingdom reality of God expressed in your workplace. *In Whose Image?* will catapult you into God's plan for your life and multiply your influence at work. Everyone who reads this will walk away with a treasure. Filled with glimpses of Andy's personal journey and loaded with biblical insights, this book will give the reader much to ponder and much to put into practice. You are heaven's representative every day and every place you go! Read this book and find your true identity. Your workplace is now the platform for your ministry!

Brian Simmons
Passion & Fire Ministries
The Passion Translation Project

A significant portion of our lives occurs at work. It is a place of community, of ministry, and a path where we walk alongside God. Andy's book is an inspirational reminder of the powerful presence of a living God in the midst of our ordinary everyday lives. *In Whose Image?* gives us significant equipping to embrace the call on our lives to love others and serve God, wherever our place of work is. What a joy to see every day as an opportunity to walk in God's purpose and presence in our workplaces! This is such a significant book.

Rachel Turner
Founder
Parenting for Faith

In Whose Image?

When you read a book like this one – with wonderful stories of faith, obedience, and God coming through in the nick of time – it's easy to wonder if they are merely good anecdotes or are truly the way the author lives. I have the privilege of praying regularly with Andy and his wife Adrienne, and without fail, every time, they are utterly committed to asking God how He sees the situation. Just like this book, it is both deeply encouraging and challenging! However, what I love most from these pages, even more than the stories, is Andy's raw honesty about the tears, tribulations and triumphs of walking by faith. Far from scaring you off, it will make you wonder whether any other way of life is really worth living.

Adam Price
Pastor
Hope Church Harrogate

In a very down-to-earth and authentic way, Andy Black shares the highs and lows of many years, during which he has endeavoured to serve God in his various places of work, reflecting a deep relationship with God and a desire to serve his king.

Each chapter allows us a glimpse into Andy's journal, giving access to moments of workplace joy, reflections on failure, and lament in some of the darkest moments. Andy also tracks moments of encouragement and insight that have spurred him forward and opened up new and effective opportunities. This is the story of a man who has looked to see the kingdom extended in his workplace in spite of multiple setbacks, and a frank and candid account of how that has worked out.

David Oliver
Author
All About Heaven
Love Work Live Life
Work Prison or Place of Destiny

Inspiring, hope-filled and wise. Bravo! Here's an 'ouch!', 'whoops!', 'yay!', 'no-o-o!', warts-and-all reflection on seeking to work with God in the ups and downs of a long career. Andy Black doesn't make a principle out of his own experience; rather he offers us the benefit of the biblical kingdom principles he's learned from his experience of seeking Christ's direction and putting Him first, whatever the cost. What emerges is not only applicable to any workplace but God-glorifying in its testimony to the Lord's faithfulness and good purposes.

Mark Greene
Mission Champion
The London Institute for Contemporary Christianity

In Whose Image? is not only well written; it is a powerful challenge. And the challenge is not just to do something; it is to be something. Andy writes like all good authors; you feel like you are having a conversation with him. But the conversation doesn't end on the last page of the book; it will lead you into action. What kind of action? Life-changing, world-changing, kingdom-impacting. I recommend you read it with your Bible close by, with not only your eyes but also your spirit; and with a mindset ready to rewrite your personal mission statement.

Rich Marshall
Author
God@Work volumes I and II
God@Rest

Acknowledgements

To
Hannah, Caroline & Rebecca,

my three wonderful daughters,
who came along for the ride and are now enjoying
their own amazing adventures with God.

I would also like to thank:

- those many special people who have been with me at crucial times along my journey when I have needed your spiritual input and friendship; you are unnamed in this book, but God knows who you are;

- my family editorial team of Adrienne, Hannah, Darren, Caroline, James, Rebecca and Daniel for your invaluable help in shaping the contents of this book; I love and appreciate you all more than words can say;

- the Onwards and Upwards editorial team for your usual care and diligence in scrutinising the manuscript and publication of the book.

Contents

In Whose Image?

Introduction

Have you ever wondered how to spiritually navigate your workplace as a Christian? Or considered the possibility that you could grow in Christ through your job's many challenges?

Work with God is a Christian ministry, founded in 2000, to help answer these questions. Its message is birthed out of God's own heart which longs to see His people live and work in close relationship with Him; to reflect His image and not be a copy of the world around them.

In these pages, I have carefully selected seven themes from my own varied working life with God to illustrate this message. I pray that you, the reader, will be inspired and encouraged to discover your unique, God-given identity and purpose in the sphere of work; that you will thereby understand who you really are and what you are supposed to be doing in this world.

'God spoke: "Let us make human beings in our image, make them *reflecting* our nature so they can be responsible for the fish in the sea, the birds in the air, the cattle, and, yes, Earth itself, and every animal that moves on the face of Earth."'

Genesis 1:26 (MSG, italics mine)

'We have become his poetry, a re-created people that will fulfill the destiny he has given each of us, for we are joined to Jesus, the Anointed One. Even before we were born, God planned in advance our destiny and the good works we would do to fulfill it!'

Ephesians 2:10 (TPT)

'We are being transformed into his image with ever-increasing glory.'

2 Corinthians 3:18b

CHAPTER ONE

Torn Between Two Kingdoms

Spiritually Navigating the World's Systems

'Beware that no one distracts you or intimidates you in
their attempt to lead you away from Christ's fullness by
pretending to be full of wisdom when they're filled with
endless arguments of human logic. For they operate with
humanistic and clouded judgements based on the
mindset of this world system, and not the anointed
truths of the Anointed One.'

Colossians 4:8 (TPT)

These are wise words from St Paul, but easier said than done!
In the world of work many spirits are competing to dominate a
Christian's life, whilst he or she tries to perform their job
competently and with a measure of satisfaction. It is a common
experience to feel torn between different choices.

My own employment journey was besieged in this way. In
this chapter we will look at some examples in which I found a
way through by *working with God*, by choosing His kingdom.
If you desire to line up with Christ's kingdom where you work,
you'll find some keys here to help.

NOT I, BUT CHRIST

For the Christian new in faith, the workplace is a perplexing environment. Having only just left one kingdom we are now trying to find our feet in another. In this spiritual world, finding the right boundaries becomes a journey of trial and error. Church fellowship becomes a vital necessity if we are to stay aligned to our new relationship in Christ.

In my early years, after a radical conversion to Christ, I worked as a freshly qualified psychiatric nurse on an NHS adolescent unit, after sensing God call me there to 'love where there was no love before'.

My trials were numerous, such as a fear of being amongst unpredictable teenagers with a range of serious problems, and colleagues grumbling incessantly, reciting countless strategies for leaving. It would have been easy to join them, but I clung on to God through sheer obedience, knowing He wanted me there.

I was also in the midst of a persistent 'secular humanist culture', meaning 'belief without God'. This spirit infiltrated the environment with godless therapies that focussed mainly on the 'self'. As such, my Christian faith was not allowed to be aired and at times was ridiculed when I spoke of it.

Whilst I probably underestimated the power of this spirit at the time, I was still aware of something coming against 'Christ in me'[1] and desperately clung on to God. Nevertheless, I suffered falls in motivation and frequently didn't want to return to work.

Along with encouragement from church life, I often processed my thoughts in a journal, which helped me work

---

[1] See Colossians 1:27.

through struggles of this kind. Frequently, God would speak as I wrote (I 'sensed' rather than 'heard'), which was of great comfort and strength to me. His perspective became clear as I wrote down my thoughts.

Here are two examples taken from my journal:

'I am crushed if I struggle on by myself, yet raised up and have God's strength when I live by the Spirit.'[2]

'This is God's work, not mine, so I'm often reluctant like Jonah and want to run away. If I don't go to be with these young people and pray, who will? Maybe it is the first time anyone has ever prayed for them. Perhaps it's their only chance of salvation. So how can I not go? Moses and Jeremiah were also reluctant in their day.'

And I prayed, 'Lord, take my life and use it for Your purposes. Help me to die to self and say, "Not I, but Christ."'[3]

God will use difficult situations at work to grow us spiritually. He is a kind father and knows what He's doing. Staying the course and not running away will help us move forward from a self-centred life to a Christ-centred one.

CHOOSING THE KINGDOM OF LIGHT

God wants us all to grow in kingdom faith so that we can bring His light into our dark workplaces. He will show us how to do it. All we need to do is listen and obey, but this doesn't mean we don't struggle with spiritual conflicts at times.

---

[2] See Galatians 5:16-17.
[3] See Galatians 2:20.

Several years into my Christian faith God moved me and my family to a church setting which embraced a deeper expression of the gifts of the Spirit. I was greatly changed, and this had an immediate impact on my working life. One consequence was an ability to discern the differences between a culture of humanism and Christ's kingdom.

Whilst nursing I was also able to teach, and I enjoyed creating lesson plans for all kinds of students. One day I was away at another hospital teaching the subject of Family Therapy to a mix of NHS professionals. It was a good experience but there was a conflict growing within me that asked, 'How can I work in a secular environment using humanistic therapies and remain uncompromising with God?' I wondered about a career change. 'Is it time to leave the NHS?' I pondered. Emboldened by a new spiritual authority, I wrote in my journal:

'All I want to do is preach the gospel!'

One evening at church I was grappling with this, wondering if I should look deeper into the origins of the models I was teaching. But God didn't agree. He said, 'That would be like looking into other religions to prove that Christianity is the right one.' Then He added this strategy: 'Just be obedient to Me and I will show you the way.' His word strengthened me, and I wrote:

'All I need is Christ. His kingdom is far greater than any theories!'

The conflict had left me doubting the work I was called to do, which in turn had stopped me praying. So, I started again: 'Lord, Your kingdom come in this place of work; keep me on the straight and narrow whilst I am here.' Then the inner conflict left me.

I had been torn between two kingdoms, Light and Darkness. God was teaching me to discern between them. When I committed to Christ's kingdom through prayer, I was delivered of the darkness. Hence the conflict left me.

> When we focus on God and not the spiritual dilemma, we are submitting to God and resisting the enemy who will then flee from us.[4] This kind of victory keeps us firmly in the kingdom of Light, performing the job God is happy for us to do. Meanwhile, we've grown a little more into His image.

PRAYING AT WORK

The exercise of prayer is a key element in our relationship with Jesus and the display of His kingdom around us.

I was always eager to pray for the young people on the adolescent unit, but the opportunities were rare. Knowing I was a Christian, some senior staff had warned me from the start, 'It's all well and good that you have a Christian faith, but don't bring it to work with you. These young people are extremely vulnerable.' Whilst I understood this and was eager to respect the clientele, I would also wait on God for opportunities that He clearly provided, aligning to sensitive scriptures such as 1 Corinthians 13:4:

'Love is patient, love is kind.'

---

[4] See James 4:7.

One evening a small group of young people returned angrily from a trip out. It was a dark, cold winter's night and the unit atmosphere was toxic due to a conflict they had brought back with them. As they struggled to cope with it, there was a lot of shouting, and a fight was imminent. So the staff introduced a 'peace intervention' that separated them to receive individual help.

I was allocated to a fifteen-year-old young man in a small private room. He sat looking at the floor with a furious expression on his face. I calmly invited him to share his problem with me, and as we talked together over a lengthy period, God revealed to me a clear vision for his issue. I 'saw' him in the middle of a field surrounded by thistles and thorny bushes.

They symbolised a spirit called 'trouble', which accompanied him wherever he went. This was a major reason why he had spent most of his life getting into trouble with various authority figures, from parents to head teachers and the police.

I shared my vision with him and asked if he would like prayer. He perked up when I said that, and so I did. As we sat there together, the Holy Spirit came gently and calmed the storm, changing his face visibly to one of peace, as he invited Jesus into his life to help him get rid of 'trouble' forever.

> This sort of opportunity for spiritual ministry at work may be rare for most of us, but with a desire to pray, a readiness to bring Christ's kingdom and a discernment to know when and how to pray, a significant impact can be achieved.

WORKING WITH UNBELIEVERS

If we work amongst people who have, as Paul describes, 'the mindset of this world system'[5], we will sooner or later find ourselves at odds with popular opinion as we do what God tells us.

When I became a Health and Social Care lecturer at a city college, I felt a strong affinity with my colleagues from day one. Despite our varied cultural and professional backgrounds, we had a shared sense of purpose, even comradeship. But then something happened to shift this cohesive position: the teaching union decided to strike over pay and conditions, and all my team agreed.

But I didn't share their concerns. I was very happy with my new work, and I was getting paid a higher salary than ever before. So I had a tough decision to make. If I agreed to join them it would preserve our friendships, if not it could undermine them and, worse, make me their enemy.

I asked God whether I should strike, hoping He'd say yes. But He clearly said no! This put me in a very awkward situation because the last thing I wanted was to be ostracised by my new team members. But I knew what God had said and was determined to remain faithful to Him.

In times of worry I imagined myself walking through picket lines, being jeered and hailed as a traitor. All I wanted to do was enjoy my work!

My stance became known, and one day I bumped into a fellow lecturer, from a different department, in the men's toilet. I was beginning to know him as a cheery fellow around college, but today I saw a different side to him. He wasn't the smiling

---

[5]   Colossian 2:8 (TPT).

man but a militant union official. As we washed our hands, he spoke to me with an undertone of intimidation via the mirror reflection.

'Hey, Andy, I didn't see you becoming a traitor to the cause!'

I was speechless, while he added:

'Well, if you do persist with your idea of working while we're striking, you could always donate your salary to the union funds.'

I had no answer to give and just awkwardly smiled and walked away, feeling like I'd just traversed my imaginary picket line.

Then as suddenly as it had arisen, the strike was called off. I was relieved beyond words, hoping for a quiet return to anonymity. But the Holy Spirit took me a step further.

Unrest amongst the staff remained, as impending government cutbacks in colleges across the country alarmed them. Meanwhile, I was working 'unto the Lord'[6] and very happy to be in the sort of employment I'd dreamed of for years. So one day, full of the Spirit and in the absence of rational thinking, I was inspired to comfort the fearful staff with these words:

'Don't fret, for Jesus is Lord. Andy Black'

I wrote it out on a slip of paper, photocopied it and placed one inside each of the hundred pigeonholes in the general staffroom. When I later gave some thought to what I'd done on the spur of the moment, I cringed with dread, fearing dire consequences.

---

[6] Colossians 3:23.

However, God's purposes unfolded the next day when two Christian staff approached me. They thanked me for the spiritual encouragement, and we all decided to start a regular prayer group for the college. Our role as intercessors commenced the following week and continued for many months.

> When we are working in step with the Holy Spirit, we can have a natural response to something performed in the supernatural. Elijah reacted similarly in fear of Jezebel.[7] When we choose to listen and obey God, we will develop our distinctive 'in Christ' identity, which can influence others too.

STANDING FIRM

High pressure is a cultural norm in many work environments. The spirits of fear and intimidation are never far away, as I discovered a few months into my new lecturing post.

While I loved most aspects of the job and worked hard to achieve high student success, I was not prepared to toil at the expense of my health, family life or indeed my soul. But my female team leader was an extremely driven person, and our difference of approach led to an inevitable clash. Alone in the office together one afternoon, she confronted and accused me of not being a team player. Pinpointing a certain member of staff as her perfect example, she said, 'I want you to be more like her. She rarely leaves the office before 6pm and is always willing to do things to strengthen the team.'

---

[7]   See 1 Kings 19:3.

Rather stunned, I patiently listened to all her demands, and didn't respond with a word. I didn't know what to say!

Later I discovered that my male predecessor in this team had quit with an illness due to stress. Likewise, other college lecturers who 'bent their knee to the system' were succumbing to horrible stress-related diseases such as ME.

As for me, I sought the Lord and gave it over to Him, finding His peace in doing much as I had before, focussing on my students and their success.

'Let the peace of Christ [the inner calm of one who walks daily with Him] be the controlling factor in your hearts [deciding and settling questions that arise].'[8]

This clash of kingdom cultures didn't bode well for my future as a lecturer. As the end of the academic year, and my short-term contract of one year, came into view, I grew nervous at the thought of unemployment.

I felt the struggle in a system where the employee must survive through compromise, where friendships are paramount and the salary at the end of the month even more so. But scarily, I was of a different spiritual culture. Pleasing God is the top priority in Christ's kingdom, and being in this position I discerned a conflict of kingdoms most keenly. I had started well and had become proficient as a teacher; but I had collided with the establishment, that is, the spiritual, political and competitive aspects of college life. As such, my position within this system was becoming precarious.

One late afternoon in June, I awaited my fate as I sat with my manager in an empty classroom, her mood unsurprisingly

---

8   Colossians 3:15 (AMP).

negative. She reeled off a carefully selected list of wrongdoings then left me hanging on to my job by a thread. Like a judge awarding a stay of execution to a prisoner on death row, she declared solemnly, 'I've decided to give you a further six-month contract, to be extended if things improve.'

I breathed a sigh of relief and said, 'Thank you.'

Now the end of term, the college deserted of students, the voluminous amounts of paperwork done and tidied away, I went on vacation with my family. Then I returned invigorated in September and flung myself back into the teaching I so enjoyed. But it was hard to shed the six-month 'cloud' hanging over me and the sense of uncertainty stuck to it. So I sought God's help and He urged me to 'stand firm'.

It was short and simple, but it strengthened my resolve.

Often God's words to us seem too brief to be of help. But He is the Master of the 'simple and profound'. The wider meaning of His instruction was this: I was to 'stand firm' upon His Word and ways, not those of people. Ephesians 6:10 (TPT) expands this wonderfully: 'Be supernaturally infused with strength through your life union with the Lord Jesus. Stand victorious with the force of his explosive power flowing in and through you.'

This did hold me firm, and as the academic year rolled forward beyond Christmas, my manager awarded me another six-month extension that took me to the end of my second college year, which flowed like the first but with deeper job satisfaction. She then granted me another one till March.

With my hopes ascending with each six-month increment, and standing firm on God's 'solid ground', I returned to college confidently after the summer holiday. I was refreshed and ready to work through my latest contract. But ill news awaited me. The government had enforced budget cuts, just as the staff feared. This left our department with more staff than finance, which meant that several lecturers, including me, were elected to apply for the limited full-time jobs made available.

My interview was straightforward, and I enjoyed it, but with the shortened contract arrangements I sensed that my manager would use this occasion to finally cut the thread. And so it proved to be. After a nervous wait of several days, while all the interviews were conducted, I finally received an impersonal phone call from her at work that confirmed my suspicions. I didn't get a job.

Now that she'd shut the door to me on her own department, my manager then proposed a solution. Upbeat in manner, she said to me, 'Here's the deal, Andy: accept two half-time jobs in other departments or take voluntary redundancy.' A very persuasive lady, she strongly recommended I accept the jobs.

But alone in God's presence later, I began to doubt her view. I could see clearly that it was a bad idea since these two posts would not complement each other and I was not prepared to do two jobs poorly. Yet without them I was staring redundancy in the face, and to me that was a portrait of horror!

After nineteen years of continuous full-time employment, it felt like a dreadful failure and, worse, it left me with a blank space where something very precious was inscribed: 'Work Identity'. It also left me with this huge question: 'How will I support my family and pay the house mortgage?'

I agonised for many days. It was like 'wringing my hands' over something with a life-or-death sentence. After many sleepless nights I had no clear word from God. He was annoyingly silent!

Then one evening, out of sheer desperation, I phoned my church leader. I explained my dilemma and made a frantic plea for wisdom. After giving it some thought, he said, 'Sometimes it's the right thing to leave a situation.'

His simple words dropped a prophetic plumbline of truth into my heart, and I knew in that moment what to do – accept voluntary redundancy – and, very importantly from God's viewpoint, this decision did not carry a stigma of failure. Clearly, He had something better in mind for my future.

> With reference to the wisdom expressed by King Solomon in Ecclesiastes 3:1-8, there's also a right time to stay and a right time to leave. Accepting God's truth was a defining moment in my relationship with Him. Trusting God against others' strong advice (particularly testing when they are in a senior management position over us) is the way forward to receiving the 'mind of Christ' and, with it, His kingdom.[9]

So, at the age of forty-one, my full-time lecturing career ended with a small redundancy payout. My trusting heart now said to God, 'Over to You!'

He didn't let me down.

At the start of the New Year, I had no full-time work, but neither was I unemployed. In fact, I didn't even leave the college. To my surprise I was offered various bits and pieces of training work from my previous department.

---

[9] 1 Corinthians 2:6-16.

> God's purposes for us cannot be thwarted despite spiritual altercations. As Psalm 33:11 declares, 'The plans of the Lord stand firm for ever, the purposes of his heart through all generations.'

I could sense God orchestrating my working life, as if each aspect were the piece of a jigsaw puzzle. This represented a portfolio of work relating to my skills and qualifications of helping and teaching, to which He just kept adding and adding, making the whole picture bigger.

The next piece then came along. Whilst lecturing, I had gradually begun to miss the hands-on work of a carer and looked to counselling to fulfil this, rather than a return to my previous career of psychiatric nursing.

There was a counselling service in the college for students and staff, with one counsellor. Early in the spring term this position became vacant, and I applied since it was the perfect fit for me with my unique psychiatric experience and Counselling Certificate that I had providentially gained two years earlier. God had prepared me well.

The interview was like a fast-flowing river on a hot summer's day. God's presence was all over it, and I was offered the job with big smiles all round.

There had been nothing to worry about!

As Jesus taught:

> 'Seek first his kingdom and his righteousness, and all these things will be given to you as well.'[10]

> Our imposing workplaces can terrify us at times with their high demands and expectations, but God is not

---

[10] Matthew 6:33.

only greater than anything; His perfect love holds us securely in the palm of His hand. As we traverse the storms, He is with us and will take us through, often with surprising outcomes.

KEYS

1. Choose which kingdom you will serve and stick to it. God is faithful to help.

2. Align with what God wants by dying to self in every situation.

3. Declare God's words, scriptural and prophetic, frequently over your working life.

PRAYER

Father God,

Thank you for my work and the rewards it brings.

Please strengthen my resolve when it all gets too hard.

Help me, Lord, to be sensitive to Your presence as I progress through each day.

I declare, Your will be done, Your kingdom come in this place as it is in heaven.

In Jesus' name,

Amen.

CHAPTER TWO

The Mysteries of God

All's Well that Ends Well

'I don't think the way you think.
The way you work isn't the way I work.'

Isaiah 55:8 (MSG)

If we choose to live by faith, alongside God's Spirit in our jobs, we should expect to encounter circumstances that make no sense at all. Whilst we may fret and weep in our bewilderment on this journey, the hope remains that when the trial ends it will make perfect sense. For there does come a time when the mind finally catches up with the Holy Spirit. And what a relief that is, for we realise (and perhaps not for the first time) that our Father in heaven does know what He's doing after all!

During my psychiatric nursing career, I faced the pressure of adhering to the system's ladder of success in the form of promotion to management. I never felt comfortable with my work identity being moulded towards this but, unable to resist, was caught up in its grip for several years.

Whilst a 'system person' succeeds or fails in a worldly culture, a 'spiritual person' (in Christ) by contrast can find themselves on a very different journey of identity, though they may not know it at the time.

One day, during my time on an adolescent unit, my boss persuaded me to attend a three-day course for aspiring managers, which I did. I was fascinated by the theoretical models presented and even went as far as planning a future career path to focus on management. I was feeling a little more comfortable and naturally looked to God to provide me with this sort of job, in line with His purposes for my working life.

At the same time, my wife Adrienne and I sensed that God was about to expand our horizons, as He had given us this directional prophecy: 'There is a whole world out there and the current job is just one small step towards it.' Psalm 37:4 reinforced this:

'Delight yourself in the Lord
And he will give you the desires of your heart.'

I was gripped by this exciting future and, when I soon discovered a job advertisement in the *Nursing Times*, thought I'd found it. The advert seemed to jump out at me! It described a junior management position at a psychiatric adolescent unit in a city sixty-five miles from home. The perfect situation seemed to have presented itself to me.

When God speaks a directional word into our lives, and events seem to line up, we can become very confident that we know what's going on. But our calculations can be far off the mark because we are not discerning events from God's perspective but our own.

I arranged a visit and found myself in a very run-down industrial area of Lancashire. It was a far cry from our pretty rural village in Yorkshire. The premises were dilapidated, but I was informed that it would be undergoing a substantial refurbishment and a fresh recruitment of staff, after serious issues had shut down the unit five months earlier. I saw this as a great opportunity for me to input lots of fresh, creative ideas into this vacuum. But was this God's job for me?

That night in bed I turned out the light, lay on my back and complained to God, 'What a rabbit warren that unit is!'

In reply, God had me look beyond the bricks and mortar into the hearts of the adolescents.[11]

I began to cry as I saw their anguish and yearning for God. Someone needed to go and tell them about Jesus. It was severe crying from God's heart through me,[12] with tears rolling out of the sides of my eyes, yet somehow I was emotionally detached from it.

Then God said to me, 'I have been preparing you and you are now ready.'

'Ready at last,' I thought, 'after all this time. But I don't *feel* ready!'

Then a dawning realisation crept over me as I began to think about all I would leave behind, like my home, church and friends, and I now began to sob for myself. These were now my own, grieving tears. It was the pain of loss, and a struggle arose between my needs and God's purposes.

---

[11] See 1 Samuel 16:7.
[12] See Romans 8:26.

By the time morning arrived, peace had finally come. Reconciled to His Spirit, I said to God, 'I will go,' reasoning that there would be even better things ahead.

I was reminded of Acts 16:9, where Paul has a vision in the night, seeing a man over the border in Macedonia crying out, 'Please help us.' His immediate reaction was to go, concluding that God had called him to preach the gospel to them.

> We don't know what's in us until God deals with the contents of our heart. It's like spiritual surgery and can emotionally catch us unawares during times in His presence. It's a serious business, like all surgery, and removes and repairs things blocking spiritual progress.

I sought the advice of a church leader, who said, 'Continue to consult God. Don't uproot your family for the sake of a job whose incentive may just be the excitement of promotion.'

The next day Adrienne saw a vision whilst we were praying. It was a space rocket, symbolising the purpose of God for us. There were parts falling off the vessel, representing people and things to leave behind as we moved forward towards our destiny. But we were off, and nothing could stand in our way. This strengthened us to believe this statement I wrote down:

> 'We are "called according to his purposes" and "if God be for us, who could be against us?" (Romans 8:28-31).'

I was becoming so convinced this move was right that I applied for the post, and even fearlessly shared the whole story with some work colleagues. Sure enough, the letter arrived inviting me to attend for an interview three weeks later.

Then along came another confirmation, this time related to our church. A leader phoned, informing us that a new pioneering venture was underway in the very same area where the adolescent unit was based. I contacted them and was excited by their invitation to visit the following weekend.

Adrienne and I stayed over with a warm-hearted couple, and on the Sunday morning the evangelistic leader shared a prophetic word for us: 'I see your heart and I love what I see because of your obedience to Me. Although in front of you there seem to be immovable mountains, know that I am an immovable mountain. I can crush anything in your way and make it clear. Because of your obedience to My calling, you will perform miraculous things in My name.'

On returning to our own church, we felt an odd detachment, reasoning that our 'heart' was now a pioneering one in Lancashire.

On the morning of the interview, Adrienne and I travelled across together. It was a bright, warm day and I felt quietly confident. We arrived at the rather beaten-up adolescent unit, and I left my wife sitting in the car, praying.

There were three people on the interview panel – two men and a woman who was the human resources (HR) manager. We huddled together in a small, shabby room and chatted across a stained coffee table. I was fairly calm and even enjoyed the occasion, and was told to expect the decision by phone call that evening.

Afterwards the kind couple from the church that'd we'd stayed with gave us a tour of the local housing and schools in the area with a view to us living there. Then we journeyed back with a satisfaction as to where our future lay.

I had a nervous wait at home that dragged on till 8pm. Then the phone rang, and I picked up with expectancy. It was the HR manager and she told me that *I hadn't got the job.*

I was stunned but found the presence of mind to ask, 'Then who *did* get the job?'

'Nobody,' she replied.

'But why?' I pressed her for a reason, becoming more confident in my dismay.

Unwillingly, she replied, 'Err... well, really it is because there was no one on the panel with the authority to choose a candidate.'

At this point I ran out of things to say and ended the call with a quiet, 'Thanks for letting me know.'

I put down the phone, dumbfounded.

When I shared the news with Adrienne we couldn't speak for a while, our minds trying to get a grip on the situation. We slumped down on the sofa, gazing down at the carpet in disbelief. Then we started analysing this odd situation.

Why had there been so many positive signs? Hadn't God clearly implied that this is what He'd planned? What about all the reassurances from mature Christians? What was going on at this unit?

When we had recovered some composure, we prayed together, only to be shocked again – this time at God's reaction.

He said, 'Why are you so downcast? I am laughing. Now, laugh with Me for I am God and I can do anything. Nothing is impossible for Me. If I tell a mountain to move, it moves. Look to Me, for in My presence is fullness of joy, whatever the circumstances.[13]'

So, we did. Somehow, He enabled us to laugh and laugh until our sides ached. It was quite bizarre!

---

[13] See Psalm 16:11.

This was a Holy Spirit 'supernatural' moment, because in the natural there was absolutely nothing to laugh about! By this mysterious action, God enabled us to come into His world by faith, rather than stay in ours.

Yet this was not the end of the matter.

Four days later I was suffering with depressive thoughts, my life darkened by what I perceived as failure, when God seemed to rally us to have another go. 'Believe and receive!' He said.

This gave us a welcome sense of His peace and we realised that, since nobody had been offered the position, it remained vacant. We believed that God had promised me this job and that He would honour His word.

This was confirmed a few days later when a church friend phoned, knowing our situation, and stirred us to take further action. He strongly suggested, 'Don't just sit back and wait for something to happen. Go and possess the land!' and he called it a 'Joshua moment'[14].

The next day he helped me to compose a 'letter of intent' to the HR manager, seeking another interview with an appropriate panel in order to explain my vision for the adolescent unit more fully. He encouraged me to write it confidently, on my terms, and to state that I would be contacting her shortly with a follow up phone chat.

It all seemed rather brash to me. I felt more shoved than encouraged, so when I popped the letter into the pillar-box I did so with a 'help me' prayer.

This posted letter, sent first class, began a sequence of events, something like trying to batter a door down! Three days later I rang through my 'follow up' phone call to the manager.

---

[14] See Joshua 1.

But she was on holiday and would be back the next day. So I left a message with her secretary.

I felt like a man 'on a roll', determined to push through, so when I heard nothing back, I phoned the day after on a Friday whilst at work, only to discover that the HR department was closed until the following Tuesday due to the bank holiday.

By then I would be away all week on holiday myself, and I wasn't going to deal with work issues then. My 'roll' within me was slowing against this resistance, so I sought God about it.

'You taught me long ago not to strive,' I said strongly, and then questioned Him, 'Am I striving now? Is this job my own selfish desire that's not working out because it's contrary to Your will? Or are You teaching me perseverance and hard work?'

I heard nothing back, just like my phone calls!

So I left for our family holiday, just having to trust God.

> When we've done everything we can possibly do, and God is silent, it's time to lay things down and trust Him. There's nothing else we can do. Such is the mystery of the faith journey.

On my return, I pressed in again and finally tracked down the elusive HR manager. But her reply profoundly exasperated me. She informed me, 'The decision has been taken to shut down the unit for good, so there won't be any more interviews.'

'Oh,' I said, the wind taken out of my sails. Now there was no longer a door to break down! I quietly said goodbye for the last time.

Soon after, we contacted the church in Lancashire to explain our bewildering situation. They were as disappointed as us and we said another last goodbye. It looked like our pioneering days were over before they'd even begun.

Totally baffled and emotionally drained by the last few months, I demanded of God, 'What on earth has all this been about?'

Thankfully, God was swift to revive me. As Adrienne and I prayed, He repeatedly called out my heavenly identity: 'Man of God, man of God, man of God, stand tall. Do not look to the right or the left but trust in me. As I have been in you, that is all that is required.'

> God's timing is impeccable. Reviving our heavenly identity gets to the very core of where we need strengthening, more so than understanding our circumstances. Identity transcends knowledge on a journey of mystery.

Back on my own adolescent unit, I settled into a familiar work pattern, unable to explain to my colleagues why I was still there! However, once strengthened in my identity, the confusion began to melt away when circumstances shifted. Through a series of events over an eighteen-month period, I finally realised what God had meant by His promise of 'new horizons'. These culminated in a house move to a beautiful town in North Yorkshire to be part of a pioneering church. Also, my work was no longer in psychiatry but education, where a long-held dream was realised. All this was totally unexpected. God had firstly mystified, then surprised and delighted us with His plans. Such are the mysteries of God at work.

Mystery can be a hard road to walk, but unless we do things God's way, however bewildering, we will not become who He says we are nor do the things He's planned for us. 'Isaiah's question, "Is there anyone around who knows God's Spirit, anyone who knows what he is doing?" has been answered: Christ knows, and we have Christ's Spirit.'[15]

---

[15] 1 Corinthians 2:16 (MSG).

KEYS

1. Working with God, by faith, often takes us beyond what we can rationally understand with our minds.

2. Struggling with some mystery is inevitable.

3. Sticking it out till the end has rewards for purpose and personal growth.

PRAYER

Father God,
I am so blessed that You know and understand me perfectly.
This enables me to trust You with my daily life.
Thank you for calling me to do my work with You.
Teach me Your ways.
Help me to persevere under the trial of not knowing and lead me forward into Your purposes and my growth.
For Christ's sake,
Amen.

CHAPTER THREE

Holding on to God

Trust is a Must

'I press on to take hold of that for which Christ Jesus took hold of me.'

Philippians 3:14

There is a rainbow of promise over every one of God's children, however difficult our journey may be at times. Keeping hold of Him by trusting His ways will keep us on track whilst enjoying the thrill of growing into the image of Christ.

Failing at job interviews is a risk we all take, and it's hard to bear. But cheer up! Failure is not how God sees it. During my psychiatric nursing career, I endured several long months of attending interviews for management positions, whilst failing every time.

I was quite philosophical about these disappointments and wrote in my journal:

'I'm going through a process of transformation to become who God says I am. Like Jeremiah 1:11-12, this is what I see: each interview shifts me a little nearer to where He wants me to be.'

> God is a good Father who grows us through our trial
> and error, restoring us steadily into the image of Christ.
> As Hebrews 12:10 puts it, 'God disciplines us for our
> good, in order that we may share in his holiness.'

As I came closer to God, I received His encouraging
words,[16] urging me to see His bigger picture, indicating that a
new season was dawning. He said, 'You are about to come into
something new that you have not experienced before. You
don't need to strive, but it is vital that you spend time solely
with Me.'

When another management position arose and I failed to
get this one too, there was a very different end scenario from
all the others. When the formal proceedings were over, a panel
interviewer took me to one side and quietly suggested an
alternative career move, in line with a new government
initiative called 'Care in the Community'. Long-term patients
in psychiatric hospitals were being rehabilitated to leave the
institution so they could live an independent life supported by
NHS community staff. She suggested I could apply for a job
within this team as a Community Psychiatric Nurse (CPN). So
I attended an interview and was offered the post that same day.

Later, I went for a walk alone with God, by a river in the
Yorkshire Dales in bright sunshine, and He again spoke of new
things: 'Open your eyes and see what is to come.'

I responded by singing, 'Open my eyes, Lord, I want to see
Jesus.'

It was a wonderful moment, feeling so close to God with a
new and exciting future ahead.

---

[16] See James 4:8.

> A close relationship with Jesus as King is an essential ingredient for the establishment of His kingdom at work. As we hold on to His directional words, they will help us stay on track.

My new post got off to a flying start, initially shadowing the CPN whom I was replacing. There were lots of clients to visit and I enjoyed the freedom of being out and about after the confining restrictions of the hospital environment.

I also enrolled on a Counselling Certificate course, released from CPN work for one day a week. It seemed an obvious qualification to get since counselling skills were practised all the time in my psychiatric nursing career. The official certificate would enhance my CV for future work.

> This 'piece of paper' was to be highly significant in the years to come. Sometimes the small steps we take become great leaps in the purposes of God in our lives.

While I was happily investing in the future each Tuesday, my 'flying start' as a CPN on the other four days was crash-landing.

When I first started, it was very fulfilling to visit and support clients in their homes or day hospitals. They suffered from disorders such as long-standing schizophrenia and bi-polar illnesses. I would administer medication and at other times check up on their general welfare, but overall I found great satisfaction in getting to know them and their immediate carers.

There were difficulties and frustrations too, such as actually finding the clients' homes. With no sat nav in those days, I relied on the A-Z city map book that was almost as essential to

CPN work as my knowledge of mental illness! I lost count of how many times I drove up and down a street looking for a new address, only to eventually find it in a most obvious place.

It was a struggle to adapt to this new expansive working environment and caused me some anxiety at times. So I naturally looked for the same kind of team support that I'd received in my previous work area. But I discovered a very different experience with my new colleagues. I had felt a discomfort in their company from our first introduction but couldn't explain why. They were an all-female, close-knit multi-disciplinary unit that had worked together for several years. I'd replaced the only man in the team in order to work with male clients. One thing I did suspect was that the most senior person (and probably group leader) disliked me from day one.

The only other CPN in the team was my line manager, whom I met up with every week for supervision. She was a woman with a strong work ethic and drive for perfection that offered very little leeway for error. As such, a spirit of condemnation was never far away. Whenever we met, I was usually accused of something that would take me by surprise. I seemed unable to do right for doing wrong in her eyes.

She would pick me up on a myriad of issues ranging from travel arrangements to paperwork, delays in communication (no mobile phones then) to appointment timing – and a big bone of dissatisfaction was team objectives which, apparently, I was failing to grasp. Try as I might, little could I do to convince her that my work, which I was mostly enjoying, could meet her, or indeed the team's, exacting standards.

I was falling short of them merely by attending the counselling course once a week, leaving me to squeeze client work into the remaining four days. Team interaction took a lowly third place!

But during this discomfort, God helped to shift my spiritual eyes once again onto His bigger picture. One Sunday at church a group of men prayed over me to be equipped at work, confirming much of what God was doing in me: 'You will be called Repairer of Broken Walls.'[17]

> We can all feel alone at work, surrounded by forces apparently intent on our destruction! The comfort of the love and spiritual strength of fellow believers is crucial. Their prophetic words have the ability to lift us up into the heavenly realm of our future, seeing beyond the current mess, at least for a while; though holding on to the comfort of this place can be hard to achieve once we return to the battle.

I was catching little sleep due to stress. Awake at 4am one morning, feeling deeply vulnerable, I was doing what I often did, writing down my thoughts to make sense of them:

> 'I'm chasing my tail, rushing about, desperately asking questions. "Is this right, or is that right? I don't know any more!" Yet I am still mostly liking my new sense of freedom, planning my own time, not unduly worried as long as the client work gets done.'

I concluded that I was doing pretty well.

But the team thought differently. I further reflected in my journal:

---

[17] See Isaiah 58:12.

'My greatest struggle is adapting to this new team. I feel askew with them, not fitting in or listened to, shut off and closed down.'

Then a team-building training day confirmed this and proved to be the 'last gasp' effort to rescue this failing relationship. It turned out that after five months in the job, nobody knew my capabilities or me personally. I felt desperately isolated. A group sculpt (to give insight into relationship dynamics) revealed that I was outside the group, looking beyond to the clients whom I felt most comfortable with, a very accurate portrayal.

This clarity lifted an unbearable intensity amongst us, but any smiles of relief were superficial and to be short-lived as the dark clouds quickly regathered after the event. There was no way forward. And the final days proved this. My supervision sessions just got emotionally draining, with more unexpected accusations thrown at me out of the blue. I remained willing to learn, but feedback persisted in being tiresomely picky and negative. With misunderstandings and confusion growing by the day, I began to doubt my sanity!

Events finally reached a brick wall one morning when I was called in to face the senior management team. Their grim demeanour said it all. They announced that from their point of view the job hadn't worked out as hoped and it was time to bring it to an end. I sat there feeling the vicious inner pain of humiliation, set against innumerable odds. I had to agree with their assessment, knowing that my position was untenable, and to move back graciously to the hospital from where I'd come.

Later I wrote in desperation:

'God, You know what's happening.'

It was a relief to receive His strategy straight back, as He reiterated the bigger picture yet again: 'Look at the purpose and plan, not the pain.'

> Paul gives us a key to this strategy in Colossians 3:2: 'Set your minds on things above, not on earthly things.' Can you see that however hopeless a situation we may find ourselves in, God wants to bring us hope from heaven? Our part is just to stay holding on to Him.

In my final hours as a CPN, I was sitting in the car having a sandwich lunch, in between last client appointments, and happened to be parked on the same street near the church where my wife Adrienne and I had wondrously encountered God ten years earlier when we were saved.

It was a bitterly cold and drizzly winter day with a weak sun occasionally breaking through the clouds. I looked into the distance mournfully but then, through grey, dripping trees, caught a glimpse of some colour in the sky. It was a clear rainbow. As I looked and wondered, I felt God's warm presence: 'Remember, I am a God of promise.'

That's all I needed. Tears welled up amid a rise of strength and hope to look beyond my baffling circumstances.

The Counselling Certificate became a vital key to progress later in my career when I became a college counsellor and went on to gain a Diploma to enhance my credentials. Achieving this position was much celebrated because it suited me perfectly in a way that CPN work never did. By holding on to God, I arrived at His job for me at that time in my life, which later provided essential skills for my 'Work with God' ministry.

KEYS

1. Always hold on to God whatever the circumstances.

2. Wait for His faithfulness to be outworked.

3. Celebrate when it all comes together.

PRAYER

Lord Jesus,

Thank you that You remain faithful through all times.

Help me hold on to You, even when it all seems too difficult.

Strengthen me to contend for Your promises and lead me forward into what You know is best.

Amen.

CHAPTER FOUR

Dreaming with God

Seeds for Future Growth

'For we are God's handiwork, created in Christ Jesus to do good works, which God prepared in advance for us to do.'

Ephesians 2:10

Hopes, distractions, sacrifices and miracles are components of dream-chasing. All the while God is with us; and as we contend through setbacks, growing in Christ as we do so, we will come into what He has prepared for us. This is because these dreams were most likely seeded into our hearts by God in the first place.

AGAINST ALL ODDS

Contained within our current jobs today may be the seed of a future career which is showing signs of germination. Perhaps a dream is starting to manifest itself.

An activity that enriched my working life as a psychiatric nurse was teaching. Completing my RMN nurse training had not been the end of study for me. I loved the subject matter and developed a godly conviction that I could do more than just practise my 'helping' art; I could also teach it, and this became my dream job.

Our deepening relationship with God enables us to see what He has waiting for us. It's our responsibility to act upon this.

So, I enrolled on a City & Guilds Teaching Certificate course, attending part time for an academic year from September at a local metropolitan university. As this went along, I initiated learning packages for staff on my psychiatric unit, which I found very fulfilling.

This course was almost scuppered from the start. I had amassed a fair amount of paperwork by the time my third daughter was born in November. My wife, Adrienne, remained in hospital for a few days, and I went to visit them after a day on my course. With me was a bag containing a folder with all my study work and an address book I was using to share our joyful baby news with family and friends.

With the hospital car park full, I managed to find a space down a dingy side street. Not wanting to take the bag with me, I left it in the car and hurried off to the maternity wing. Later that evening, back at home, I discovered the bag gone, realising that a thief had forced the passenger door and then shut it again and I hadn't noticed when I returned to the car in the gathering darkness.

'How can I now continue my course?' I lamented as I forced down my meagre evening meal.

Later I feverishly prayed for God's help before suffering a troubled night's sleep. But then a miracle happened.

The next evening, I returned to the hospital wondering whether to share the bad news with Adrienne, since she'd be in a delicate state. But on seeing me she smiled and said, 'I know about the theft, and everything is OK.'

I was astounded. Adrienne then filled me in on the details. A woman had contacted her parents by phoning numbers in the address book, having found my bag in a shrub along a walkway behind her home. My coursework was safe, and I could continue my studies as planned. I wept with joy and relief, praising God; He had achieved a great victory for me because this qualification, completed the following year, was vital to His plans for my working future.

> Contending for God's purposes against an enemy who is bent on thwarting them, is all part of the dream-chasing journey. But when all is said and done, we can stand with Job and say of God, 'Nothing and no one can upset your plans.'[18]

I now dreamed with God that one day I would be able to teach full time, perhaps at the local school of nursing. But this dream took four years to bear fruit because of career distractions. During this dormant period, I was pressured by the hierarchical system to apply for several management positions. I failed to get any of them.

Then, after my final attempt, I was advised by a senior manager to apply for a nursing job in the community. This felt right and I got the job, but after five months it turned out to be the wrong decision.

> As dream-chasers we are 'spiritual' people working in a world system that is trying to mould us into its own image. We need to recognise our unique journey, aligned

---

[18] Job 42:2 (MSG).

to God's purposes, and not be distracted away from them.

This career crisis woke me up to my stolen dream of teaching and I began a job hunt in earnest. This quest was given a hefty boost when a close church friend of ours prophesied that I would find God's job for me by way of a newspaper advertisement. Adrienne and I struggled to believe such a word, as it was so directional, which we had not often experienced up to then. Nevertheless, I was uplifted by it and persevered, searching in the job pages for several weeks. Then one day in my local library, I spotted it in an Educational Supplement. It read, 'Social Care Lecturer required, Further Education College, Leeds.'

It all felt rather surreal but looked the perfect fit for someone of my professional background of care with a teaching qualification. It was an exciting find and gave me the best job thrill I'd had in a long time. But my exhilaration was tinged with uncertainty as it came with a temporary contract for one year. My career to date had spanned seventeen years, all on permanent contractual bases. So there was a risk to financial security that I hadn't experienced before. Still, I pursued it because I sensed this was God's dream job for me.

A defining trait of a dream-chaser is their willingness to take risks. This is because God's backing gives them all the courage they need.

I successfully obtained an interview, and when the day came, Adrienne said, 'I feel confident about this one.'

On that tide of optimism my faithful wife straightened my tie, prayed for me and waved me off.

The college was based on the edge of the city centre, a rather shocking orange colour of 1960s' square, plain design and six levels high. From a bright, spacious foyer, I caught a lift to the fourth floor and found the Health and Social Care department, where several team members warmly greeted me. I smiled confidently and was soon following the section manager and one of her senior lecturers into a small interview room. It looked like it had been temporarily knocked together with panels of cardboard. An odd thing happened on my way into the room when I caught the fingers of my right hand in the handle-less door as I closed it behind me, such was the lightness of its frame.

'Ouch!' I exclaimed as quietly as I could, so as not to embarrass myself.

But then the stinging pain had a beneficial effect. Focussing upon it made me forget my anxiety, and I relaxed into an hour's discussion with genuine assurance, while nursing my sore fingers. The interview went very well, and having attended so many in the past few years without success, I had a good feeling about this one. I was particularly heartened as there was a promise that the job could become permanent at the end of the first year, allaying my worries of financial insecurity. The next day, our good feelings were confirmed when I was offered the job. My dream had come true at last.

> In this kind of process, we can all meander off the 'main road', but our heavenly Father is faithful to bring us back to the dream He has seeded. As we realign ourselves with it, there comes a time when we finally arrive. And what a great feeling that is!

WATER AND FIRE

We can have many dreams at once. Some can be godly, others not. Then there are those in a grey area in between whose God-seed is poisoned by selfish ambition. God must act to purify this seed, as happened to me.

Teaching was not the only alternative to nursing that I considered. An imaginary dream list also included being a bestselling author, something I'd aspired to since my teen years.

This desire resurfaced whenever my work became too difficult. I would resort to processing the situation in my journal and then wondering if I could turn my writing skills into a lucrative lifestyle.

Over the years, I'd built up a substantial volume of writings that I kept in a large folder. There was half-finished fiction (I could start a story but never finish one), some quite decent poems and various scribblings that hopefully would one day become bestsellers. I looked to various famous authors as role models.

But all this just evaporated once I was back walking in the Spirit and work was fine again. In reality this dream was an idol of delusional proportions and there came a time when God dealt with it severely.

We had moved to a new church, and its prophetic impact was so great that it began to change us radically. There was a planned bonfire night for Sunday 5th November on a large derelict plot of land behind its building. Over the weeks beforehand, the burnable material had grown higher and higher with the congregation's anticipation.

We too were looking forward to it, but also to something else happening earlier on the same day. Since being born again, our growth journey had led us to desiring baptism by full immersion, a dream which had not been possible until now. After the morning meeting, accompanied by many church members, we paraded through into a separate room where a large pool in the floor was revealed by removing its top cover. A small worship band struck up and the ceremony began. We were but two of many in a line of individuals.

As our turn came, someone suggested that Adrienne and I could be baptised at the same time. We found this idea inspirational since we had also been saved together, and eagerly agreed. Holding hands, we descended into the water, where two people assisted us to submerge and rise together, to rapturous applause and a scripture: 'Therefore, if anyone is in Christ, the new creation has come: the old has gone, the new is here!'[19]

After waiting for so many years, we were both relieved and elated to have satisfied this great longing. As we travelled home excitedly, we were looking forward to returning to church that evening for the eagerly anticipated bonfire.

I was enjoying family fun that afternoon, but as I took time aside to make a cup of tea, God gave me an instruction: 'Go to the event tonight and throw your writing folder into the fire.'

I was shocked!

This directive put me in serious conflict with God because my writings were so precious to me. They were the hope of a better life. 'Now where do I stand with "not I, but Christ"?' I groaned, referring to a commitment I had made to God recently.

My family and I duly attended that evening.

Amid the cheery crowd munching on their hotdogs, keeping warm by the blazing heat, and children playing chasing games

---

[19] 2 Corinthians 5:17.

at a safe distance away, I pondered my dilemma, the folder tucked under my arm.

Finally, after what seemed like hours, I gave in. Approaching the fire as near as I dared, the heat burning my face, I took the folder into my hands and threw it in. The flames quickly embraced my hopes and dreams, turning them into cinders in moments.

I instantly regretted it. 'Oh, my life. What have I done!' I screamed inside.

As we drove home, my small children chattering with the delights of their evening, I felt a great sorrow, as if someone close had died. But some hours later I calmed down, sat quietly with God and was able to trust that He had something better up ahead.

> Dying to self under the water and sacrificing my writings in the fire were the same thing: the old was gone, the new had come.

Many years later, I became a published author of several books relating to the 'Work with God' ministry. My writing aspirations had slowly but surely morphed from my selfish dream into His, with a far better result, reflecting the eternal image of Christ rather than the temporal bestselling authors of the world.

> Sacrifice is not an easy option for any of us, but our kind Father quickly replaces it with hope, which fortifies our courage to stay dream-chasing. Then over time we can all reach the miracle of coming into what God has prepared for us, from the fruition of those seeds planted long ago in our hearts.

KEYS

1. Dream with God.

2. Do what is practically necessary.

3. Push through to the end goal.

PRAYER

Dear Father,

Thank you that You have put dreams in my heart.

Help me to work with You to bring them to life and push through towards achieving them together.

In Jesus' name,

Amen.

CHAPTER FIVE

Having the Mind of Christ

Thinking Like God

'The person with the Spirit makes judgments about all things, but such a person is not subject to merely human judgments, for, "Who has known the mind of the Lord so as to instruct him? But we have the mind of Christ."'

1 Corinthians 2:15-16

Having the mind (or perceptions) of Christ is vital if we are to bring His kingdom presence into our working lives. The task set before us is to learn to think and act just like our King, in His image. There is a long process for us to undertake as led by the Holy Spirit, laying down our lives for Him. Over time God's confidence becomes our confidence as we see things His way. This changes our (often stubborn) mindsets, leading to His purposes being outworked, while God's Word, prophecy and visions are given to strengthen us along the way.

CONFIDENCE IS THE SPRINGBOARD

When God calls us to a particular job, it's very likely that we don't really know if we can do it at all. But we know what God has said and bravely step into an uncomfortable situation, hoping He is still with us. It's here in this place that we experience His thoughts, because we've no other way of happily getting through each day.

This is how it happened for me.

The autumn sun was unusually warm as I drove to work on my first day as a college lecturer in the morning rush. Suddenly God spoke into my nervous anxiety: 'Confidence is the springboard.'

As I received these words into my spirit, fear gave way to God's strength, which intensified as I repeated them out loud. By the time I arrived at my new workplace, I felt supernaturally charged, filled with the confidence of knowing that I was exactly where God wanted me and so could do all He'd called me to.

'To this end I strenuously contend with all the energy Christ so powerfully works in me.'[20]

I took this newfound 'energy' straight into the education culture, needing to keep all my wits about me, as my Health and Social Care team required me to 'hit the ground running' in the frenzied administrative setting of student induction week.

There were bodies everywhere and the noise was deafening! All the teaching departments were together in a large vestibule with their own sign-up tables, eager to grab as many students as they could. Each new learner represented money for their specialism and with other competitors in the city there was an aggressive battle for places.

As the 'new boy' I acted merely as a gofer, but I felt the exhilarating buzz like everyone else. If I were a car, I would say that I'd been sedately going along at a steady thirty miles an

---

[20] Colossians 1:29.

hour back at the psychiatric hospital where I'd previously worked. Now I was in the fast lane, topping seventy just to keep pace with my new colleagues' effervescent drive. It was also a time when I began to develop a healthy affinity for what was, to me, a new breed of worker – the 'college lecturer' – and happily, I felt quite at home.

This first week was also about getting orientated to my academic responsibilities. With this in mind, a meeting was arranged with a senior lecturer in my department. A quiet, measured lady in her early fifties, she was to be my mentor. This sounded very promising: someone who could support me with advice and resources in this strange new world. I sat in the office with her, cuddling a coffee whilst she carefully outlined my teaching schedule.

'First and most important is the photocopy department,' she said, surprisingly. 'This is the hub of the college because teaching means resources, and our biggest supply throughout the college are handouts, and thousands are needed every day. To get what you need when you need it, you must get along with the staff there. Then they'll do you the necessary favours ahead of others!'

'Sounds like a paper battleground,' I thought. Later I found her words to be very true, with this addition: the department was as hot as the tropics because the photocopy machines were at boiling point all day long. Such was the significance of this humid arena to the success of lecturing that it wasn't long before I was echoing the cries of other staff when the biggest crisis hit our day: 'A photocopier is down!'

Back at the meeting, she then introduced me to the course curriculum. It consisted of subjects relating to all aspects of health care across the entire lifespan of a human being from childbirth to old age and death. These would be studied with the intention of gaining qualifications that would prepare the students for work in care homes, day centres and the like. They could also be used as credentials towards further qualifications for jobs such as nursing, physiotherapy and psychology.

In addition, I would be responsible for arranging placements for all students and expected to liaise with care workplaces according to their particular career aspirations, then visiting and writing up reports.

She finished her preamble and waited for me to speak.

'It all sounds fascinating,' I said confidently, before adding, 'So, do you have the lesson plans and resources for me to do this?'

I was hoping that my predecessor might have left a large cupboard with a sign saying 'Resources for my successor' but, alas, they hadn't.

'You'll find everything you need in your local library,' she said, with a weighty assurance.

'Fine,' I said, not at all convinced.

Panic began to rise as I pondered the thought that my own resource 'cupboard' at home was empty with less than a week to go before I came face to face with my expectant students.

Then another thought came to me, and I asked, 'How will I know how well I'm doing in the classroom?'

'Oh', she said with a breezy air, 'don't worry; the students will tell you.'

'Sounds ominous,' I thought.

The meeting finished with a promise of more support when I deemed it necessary. But I got the impression that I was mostly on my own from then on.

My first week done, I returned home overwhelmed by the task ahead. During the weekend I dug out what I thought would be my scanty resources and was surprised by how much health information I had accumulated relevant to the curriculum. There was coursework from my psychiatric nurse training, then essays on education from the City & Guilds teaching certificate with lesson plans from teaching practice. Then fresh course notes from the counselling studies completed just three months previously. Here was a small but workable foundation for building my resources upon.

'Not so much "starting from scratch",' I thought, aligning myself to what God had already prepared me for.

'For we are his workmanship, created in Christ Jesus for good works, which God prepared beforehand, that we should walk in them.'[21]

And it was quite an easy task during the second week, as I did not need to teach much. Instead, there was a constant stream of administration over student enrolments, such as correct names on registers; and when we weren't doing that, I was organising warm-up games to help the students in their early relationships with each other. I'd done plenty of those exercises before in my previous jobs and courses.

These distractions gave me time to prepare for the third week when my teaching resources would be required across all classes. I set about matching my 'workable foundation' to the curriculum and found that I was even better prepared than I'd thought. As I put together lesson plans, my stress levels dropped and my enjoyment rose.

---

[21] Ephesians 2:10 (ESV).

'Hey,' I thought, 'I was born for this.' And I recalled my joy of teaching about 'adolescence' in the recent past. 'That's why I'm a college lecturer. God knows, I'm in the right place!'

By the time week three arrived, my confidence was brimming. I was ready.

As time went by, I found the workload often daunting, and I creaked under the pressure. One day my wife Adrienne and I were praying, and she saw a vision. It was a Cooling Tower being constructed of individual bricks, each one symbolising a task during the academic year. When they were laid at the right time and place, it would eventually lead to the completed tower. By this God gave me hope to persevere, knowing there was actually an end result to achieve and at each day's end I could say with confidence, 'Hooray, I've laid another brick today!' As Jesus' said:

> 'Do not worry about tomorrow, for tomorrow will worry about itself. Each day has enough trouble of its own.'[22]

Still, I was like a drowning man at times, and sought God on other strategies for survival. He taught me to stop, come up for air and rest with Him for a while before plunging back in.

Spiritual songs were birthed in those days. I'd be driving along or on a quiet walk after work and the Holy Spirit would teach me songs that brought me into God's presence. These simple yet profound ditties had names such as 'Working with Dad' and 'I want to do what You want to do today, Lord'. I continue to sing them to this day.

---

[22] Matthew 6:34.

Learning to come into God's presence is a vital strategy for working with Him.

Over time I was able to put teaching packages together very quickly. Looking out for resources from newspapers, magazines, TV and the like became a compulsive habit once I knew which topics I was to teach. I developed a sort of radar that would pick up health issues. I enjoyed gathering, putting them into a lesson plan, then watching them 'fly'. I disliked teaching from the same material because I got bored, so I'd freshen them up every so often.

I also learnt something about myself: I always over-prepared, having more than enough for one lesson, meaning that I could use some material for the next one. It was a case of keeping one step ahead, even if that step was just one day or even one hour; I was always ready for the lessons when they arrived. I generally loved being a teacher. It was like learning an art, and I became confident and proficient at it.

> Our heavenly Father knows our capabilities better than we know them ourselves. After all, He created us out of love! As we return this love and adopt His ways, we are then able to think like Him, seeing ourselves as He does. Confidence is the result, which can translate into abundant kingdom fruitfulness.

FOLLY OF THE HUMAN MIND

Getting Christ's perspective into our own minds is only half the battle. Protecting it is the other part. So what do we do when someone deems it necessary to contradict what God has clearly said to us? This happened to me one day.

After receiving my 'Work with God' ministry from God, I spent a year working out the mystery that it held and earned very little money in the process. It was a very tough season and I struggled to understand what God was doing as the Holy Spirit moved powerfully upon my life.

I attended a conference halfway through this year and at one evening meal I sat next to a respected business leader. He asked me about my work and family, and I shared some personal details about my current situation, trusting that he would bring some godly wisdom.

His comment was, 'It isn't right that your wife is the only wage-earner in your home. You are head of the family, and that position deems it necessary that you support them financially. Surely you can get a paid job with all your qualifications.'

Accusing me of laziness, he quoted from Proverbs 19:24 (AMP): 'The lazy man buries his hand in the [food] dish, but will not even bring it to his mouth again.'

I squirmed in his presence, embarrassed at my situation, finding it hard to disagree. I couldn't retort with any fine-sounding argument, so I just said, 'Thanks for your concern. I'll give it some thought.'

I felt sick, unable to finish my meal. Then I made an excuse to leave and hurried away, keen to find some quiet space alone with God.

I found a small, deserted counselling room, sat down and, head in hands, poured out my heart to God.

'I feel so bad. What just happened, Lord?'

God immediately responded, 'The man's words have just demolished some of the foundation stones we are building.'

'For no-one can lay any foundation other than the one already laid, which is Jesus Christ.'[23]

And my eyes were opened to a vision.

Before me was a field where several large stones were forming the early stages of a foundation for a building, one on top of the other. But a couple had toppled off and lay discarded on the ground. I understood that the man's words had had the power to dislodge those second-tier stones. And God kindly said, 'Shall we put them back?'

'Yes, please,' I replied.

As we did so, my upset was replaced by God's amazing peace, strengthening me once again, and I was able to forgive the man his folly.

'Jesus said, "Father, forgive them, for they do not know what they are doing."'[24]

The business leader apologised some weeks later saying he had not been in a good mental or spiritual place at the time.

Let us diligently learn to discern with whom we share our inmost godly thoughts, so that the mind of Christ within us is protected and grows into His kingdom purposes at work.

---

[23] 1 Corinthians 3:11.
[24] Luke 23:34.

DYING TO SELF

A further obstacle is that of our own unholy mindsets!

On my journey with God during that year, I was effectively getting to a place of starting my work life from scratch; that is, learning the humility to work God's way, not mine.

Whilst I was desperately trying to do the obvious things, such as earn money, which never worked out, God was confronting me with His priority.

This is because I couldn't possibly achieve His 'God ideas' unless I was transformed by dying to my 'good ideas'. It was often a painful process, involving repentance from sin that the Holy Spirit identified. This was the only way that my mind could be renewed.[25]

For me, it was like experiencing the physical process of death. Yet through it all my hope lay in the resurrection of Jesus Christ. My old working life was passing away with the new emerging. Jesus describes it this way:

> 'Whoever finds their life will lose it, and whoever loses their life for my sake will find it.'[26]

Also, during this time, it was as though a 'veil' lifted from my eyes and I saw Jesus afresh as the Vine with His Father as the gardener; anything not aligning to the mind of Christ was unfruitful so would be cut off and thrown into the fire.[27] I was sobered by this revelation and yearned to be fruitful and do all He'd called me to, however painful the process.

---

[25] See Romans 12:2.
[26] Matthew 10:39.
[27] See John 15:1-4.

Dying to self will cost us, but it is vital if we are to gain God's perceptions so we can work with Him, bearing eternal fruit through bringing His kingdom presence into our working lives.

KEYS

1. Commit to thinking just like Jesus.

2. Submit your own ideas to God.

3. Persevere through the challenges that come your way.

PRAYER

Lord Jesus,
I want to bring Your kingdom presence into my working life.
Help me to think like You, seeing things Your way.
I die to my own mindset and embrace all that You have for
me today.
Amen.

CHAPTER SIX

Identity at Work

Becoming Distinctively Me

'As Christ himself is seen for who he really is, who you really are will also be revealed, for you are now one with him in his glory.'

Colossians 3:4 (TPT)

For a person to gain a kingdom identity they must allow God to uproot them from the soil (or culture) of the world and be replanted in Christ, to discover all they truly are as a son/daughter of Father God. My own long adventure took me beyond anything I'd ever dreamed of and into a work identity I'd never heard of.

LIVING ON THE EDGE

It all started during an unusually dry spiritual season. (We all have them!) I was bored and hungered for more from my Christian life. Then one day God led me to read a book called *Living on the Edge* by Loren Cunningham (Youth with a Mission), unsuspecting that it was about to start a process that would radically change the course of my working life.

I devoured its contents, thrilled by every page as I read about the lives of young people who put themselves completely into the hands of God, out of which poured miraculous testimonies. I was gripped by their stories and became so excited by these possibilities in God that I cried out to Him, exclaiming, 'I want to see You do stuff in my life. I want to live on the edge too!'

> When we go through dry seasons like this, and nothing seems to satisfy, it may well be God's way of inviting us to go deeper. Like in the natural, hunger motivates us to want more. For me God used a book, but for others it could be a film, a blog or an inspirational church sermon.

I now waited, meanwhile working as a college counsellor.

One year on, I was driving the twenty miles home from work when the Holy Spirit began to direct my line of travel, taking me to a stylish residential area in my hometown. I parked, got out of the car, and perused my surroundings, waiting for further instructions.

These came in the form of a question when He asked, like He did to the prophet Jeremiah, 'What do you see?'[28]

It was 5.30pm. I looked around and answered, 'I see people walking back from work to their expensive houses. I see an area where rich people live.'

Then, as if satisfied that I had seen correctly and was in line with His purposes, God spoke into my future, saying, 'You will experience a "suddenly" for your next job. I will catapult you into it and there will be no looking back to your last place of work; it will be in the distant past. The new job will fit you like

---

[28] Jeremiah 1:11.

a glove and you will know it is right because you will have peace about it.'

Then God warned me about the nature of the work concerning 'riches', saying, 'Remain testifying to be rich in Me, not in material possessions. Your treasure is in heaven, not on earth.'[29]

'How will I find this job?' I asked.

'Seek and you will find, knock and the door will be opened to you,' He promised, referring to Matthew 7:7-8.

> God knows our deepest desires and hears the cry of our hearts; He will fulfil them His way and in His time. But it will probably take longer than we think.

A short time later was 23rd August, and the Lord added a strategic word. He said, 'The job will come, but don't forsake Me. Run after Me as you do in lean times; let it be your love for Me, not your need of Me. If you do forsake Me, the devil will overpower you because you are away from Me. Cling to Me, to My Spirit, move on with Me and the devil will have no part in you.'[30]

I knew this word was of vital importance in what God was doing, so I made an agreement with Him that day to do exactly as He had instructed and gave it a name: 'The 23 Aug Promise'.

From that day forth I rose one hour earlier each working day, sat in my lounge and waited on the Lord, to seek Him in love, not need. Sometimes I would feel His presence, other times not, but I persevered in the knowledge of its great significance,

---

[29] See Matthew 6:19-21.
[30] See John 14:30.

and over time my perspective and spiritual sense of the working day, and indeed my whole life, began to shift from mine to His.

> Looking to our natural fathers for only what we need will produce a very shallow relationship. A deeper bond is formed when love is central. Saying 'I love you no matter what' creates an indestructible partnership. This was what God was forming in these early days. He was building the foundation for a kingdom work that was going to endure and produce eternal fruit, with intimacy at its heart. Hence my vow of commitment.

SEARCHING FOR IDENTITY

If we are to reflect God's image at work rather than be a copy of those around us, a journey is required that demands a radical shift away from all we've known before.

Mine began two months later. I experienced the 'suddenly' that God had promised when a divine appointment led me to a Corporate Training Consultant, a sincere man of God.

When he told me about his job, something leapt inside of me and our conversation became vibrant. We ended our time on a buoyant high, agreeing to meet again soon. God had knitted our hearts together as friends and we both felt a sense of shared destiny. I came away convinced that this connection had a lot to do with God's job that would fit me like a glove.

I was eager to get back in touch, and within a few weeks he and I met again, new friends with a fresh purpose, as he introduced me to his working world and all it entailed. Thereafter, I continued my counselling work for half the week and started to explore the business realm with God during the other half, to see what would happen. I didn't really know what

I was doing or why, but I followed my friend's instructions and purchased a laptop and mobile phone.

Then I spent lots of time thinking up a business identity, based on the notion that God was calling me to training work. It seemed so obvious at the time. Finally, I gave myself the title, 'Relational Training Consultant'.

I was pretty sure that this would translate well from my health and education background into business settings such as teambuilding and customer care. My business friend hoped so too. So off I went in my smart suit and shiny black shoes to business conferences and Chambers of Trade gatherings in my local town.

For weeks I constantly strove to get paid work in line with the work identity that I'd created. I thought it could at least bring in some money to help supplement my meagre college wage, but nothing worked out that way.

It felt like something had to happen at some point, otherwise what was I doing all this for? I called it 'the agony of divine delay', often asking God the same question, 'Are You sure I am doing the right thing?'

The answer, to my great relief, was yes.

'Then teach me Your ways, Lord,' I responded. Like Moses, I wanted to learn God's ways over mine.[31]

Soon an unexpected opportunity arrived, when my new friend's company were having a recruitment drive for training consultants and I was encouraged to apply. This gave me great hope, as it looked like an open door into the future that God had waiting for me as a paid trainer.

---

[31] See Exodus 33:13.

God further strengthened my optimism when Adrienne and I prayed about it: 'Praise Me, like Jehoshaphat, because it's already done.[32] You've got the job!'

But I didn't get it!

Initially my heart plummeted. I had considered that it may be a bridge too far between my experience and the business world, but God had convinced me that the job was mine!

'What's going on?' I demanded.

He immediately responded, 'Nothing has changed. It's still yours.'

'Eh?' I replied, confused.

I couldn't figure it out, but I was desperately trying to.

I reasoned, 'This job is mine by divine appointment. So by faith I am certain to get it. But the timing is not for now.'

I thought of the aged Abraham when God told him about an 'impossible' future: that his barren wife would conceive of a son and he would father a nation. The birth of Isaac happened many years later than he'd assumed, but it did not stop him from believing it at the moment of promise.

> Have you ever noticed the gap between your understanding and what God is doing? It's called 'mystery'. We just want to comprehend, don't we? But all we can do is bravely follow our heavenly Father as He patiently guides us along the way. Frustrating as this can be, it's actually a great time to learn God's ways.

Without this job a hole remained. 'So, what now Lord?' I asked.

---

[32] See 2 Chronicles 20:1-30.

I felt a pressure to fulfil the work identity I had designed, so I picked myself up and persevered with it by venturing boldly into various business settings. It felt like acting a part in a play, yet I knew God wanted me to do it.

On one occasion there was a business conference in a local grand hotel. I had no official invitation, yet God encouraged me to go to it.

But I agonised over this instruction because I was someone who played life by the rules to feel safe, and here was God asking me to break them!

I sensed Him cheering me on: 'Be courageous and daring. Go to the conference as if you have every right to be there, because you do.'

Finally, I cracked, and through gritted teeth I drove to the location. I parked nearby, then, standing on God's word, ventured forth with much trepidation. Looking the part but fearing the consequences, I entered the hotel with a pretentious air of confidence, only to bump into a former student from my local counselling skills course who just happened to be walking by in the foyer. He greeted me like a long-lost acquaintance and, while I tried to gather my presence of mind, ushered me into a glamorous dining hall.

Being late I had missed the main course but was invited to partake of dessert and coffee. He led me to a seat where I was greeted by people I already knew, lots of them from church and business connections. I felt quite at home, my fears all forgotten. Not having a ticket just didn't seem to matter at all.

After the meal we all paraded through into another room where networking ensued amid a backdrop of business marketing stands. It was surreal. I was truly stunned by how God's invitation had worked out. I stepped aside from the noisy crowd and quietly phoned Adrienne on my new mobile phone, excited to share what was happening. I was living on the edge by seeing God orchestrate His miracles.

> What I didn't know, God did. All I had to do was listen, trust and obey. But it wasn't always easy!

Great moments like this were frequently overshadowed by dry spells, when nothing seemed to work, however hard I tried. I saw opportunities around me and tried to push doors that fitted with my work identity design. I wrote a proposal for customer care training for a pharmacy shop in town but heard nothing back.

I became desperate and even tried work areas that had nothing to do with corporate training, such as setting up a counselling practice and working for a crisis centre. This led to a telling off when God said, 'Don't get a job just for the money.' I didn't even know I was thinking that way!

Waiting on God one morning, He gave me a gracious promise that has established me upon His provision ever since: 'No matter how long it takes or how many mistakes you make, I will supply your needs. So do not look to money but to Me, for in Me is everything you need. Cling to Me as you would cling to a vessel on the water to save yourself from drowning.'

I desperately wanted to transition God's way, but the mindset change required evolved painfully. As long as God was in charge and I knew this beyond all reason, I was happy to play my part while He played His. But it didn't often make sense.

I was reminded of God's utter faithfulness as I journeyed along a very steep learning curve, underpinned by my '23 Aug

Promise' to continue seeking Him in love, not need. That close relationship was at the heart of our work together.

> Even more than His love, what really helped me feel secure was recognising that He fully understood me.[33] This means that whatever we go through, as long as we know that it's our Father taking us there, all will be well. He's got it in hand and success in Christ is the guaranteed agenda.

> Then God showed me how He defines success.

THE TRUE MEASURE OF SUCCESS

It is common to believe that success is linked to qualifications and performance levels at work, but in truth this thinking is detrimental to the growth of our kingdom identity. God now challenged this mindset in my own working life.

The glamorous receptionist looked up from her computer screen and smiled. 'Good morning, sir, and welcome to the conference. Would you like to register?'

'Yes, please,' I replied.

I was attending one of the largest business conferences in the country, in my hometown. I had picked up their advertising leaflet at a recent business event and became convicted that God wanted me there.

So here I was, surrounded by the hubbub of confident people in their posh business attire, networking easily with each other. I, in contrast, didn't know who I was in this work setting. I felt like an intruder or undercover spy, and I suppose I was, in

---

[33] See Psalm 139:1.

biblical terms, spying out the land. Being a man of mystery made me very nervous indeed. Anything could happen!

She continued, 'Just pop your name, business title and organisation on the form, and I'll print off an ID badge for you.'

She handed it to me. I took it but then froze.

'OK. Just give me a moment,' I said embarrassed, and awkwardly moved away to a nearby table, relieved to get some time to think.

What should be printed on the label? I wasn't sure who I was, and I wasn't part of any organisation, so what would go in that space on the form?

'At least I know my own name!' I thought, and smiled to myself.

Then I had an idea. I put a hand in my jacket pocket and pulled out a homemade business card, one of several waiting expectantly in the hopeful darkness. Then I copied my title onto the ID form.

That was fine but, 'Whom do I work for?' I asked myself.

Then I thought of something: 'I'm independent, just like a politician would be with no party allegiances.'

So in the end, 'Andy Black, Relational Consultant, Independent' went on my badge.

What I didn't know was that other delegates take an active interest in badge details, looking for networking opportunities. It happened to me when I was queuing for a fringe-training event. Another delegate saw my badge and pointed at it, asking, 'What's independent?'

Taken aback I blurted out, 'Not belonging to anyone else; on my own, you know.'

'Oh,' he sneered, 'you're freelance!'

'Err, yes,' I replied as confidently as I could, and we both knew I didn't have much idea what I really was!

I carried my embarrassment into a bright but rather cramped event room where business psychologists, human resource managers and other titled professionals paraded their expertise in discussion groups. I merely people-watched, feeling very small and out of place.

For the rest of the conference, I explored the many business stands, whilst resisting the enticement from glamour girls who pushed their marketing leaflets my way. But I came across nothing like a work opportunity, and my business cards all remained where they were, unrequited. I returned home intimidated and confused, unsure of what God wanted me to achieve.

That night I lay awake wondering about it all and challenged God saying, 'I don't understand! Who am I to be at such a conference? I'm a misfit. Everyone is more intelligent, better qualified and more successful than I am.'

God countered my bewilderment saying, 'You are in exactly the right place, even if others think you are not.' And He roared with laughter!

I found myself laughing too, convicted in His presence by the certainty that He was absolutely right. But I didn't understand why. So God explained it to me.

He reminded me that when Jesus turned up in His day, the religious people didn't think He was in the right place either, because He was not like them. Yet the truth was that He was doing exactly what His Father wanted.[34]

---

[34] See John 5:19.

This revelation suddenly transported me into a place of knowing Jesus better with a wonderful sense that I had indeed been successful.

And God affirmed me, saying, 'Yes. Success starts with knowing Jesus.'

> Can you see that success in the world is very different from success in the kingdom of God? Because God loves us without conditions, we can live *from* approval, not *for* it. Our start-point for being fully accepted is not in our achievement but from our alignment as sons and daughters in-Christ.

HEAVEN COMES TO VISIT

Just four days later, in the middle of the night as I lay in bed, God spoke to me in a loud voice, saying, 'Take the message of Christ to the business and working community.'

I got the impression that a herald angel had spoken these words and then flown off elsewhere to deliver other messages. But what held my attention more than anything was the firm conviction that God had birthed a ministry in me. I had never experienced anything like it before. It felt like I had been offered a job straight from heaven!

Also, that night God deposited in me an urgent necessity to read the Bible in a way that would communicate its substance to the workplace. Only the original Word of God would do for this 'message', with no other sources, and it would have to be readily transferable for others to apply to their work.

He also emphasised His personal presence over worldly business principles, something I had been practising since my promise to Him on 23rd August.

Jesus' words rang true:

'I am the Vine, you are the branches. When you're joined with me and I with you, the relation intimate and organic, the harvest is sure to be abundant. Separated, you can't produce a thing.'[35]

Spiritual encounters such as this are so rare that they capture our attention immediately. There are many biblical examples, from Moses and the burning bush to Saul stunned by Jesus on the way to Damascus. Whenever they occur, God's intention is to impact our lives on an unimaginable scale.

Having received this commission, I gave it the identity, 'Message Ministries', then God propelled me forward at high speed. In just three weeks a dramatic sequence of events led to a whole new world opening up to me.

One evening I attended a Christian worship event at my local church. I sat next to an elderly man, not a regular member of the congregation, who said he was there in place of his son who was in hospital. On enquiring further, he told me an extraordinary tale. His son had gone skydiving with a friend, and as they leapt from the airplane the friend's parachute failed to open and the father said that his son quickly wrapped himself around his friend and pulled the ripcord of his own chute, which thankfully opened and they both landed together on the ground. Unfortunately, the man's son dislocated both shoulders, but his friend was alive and miraculously unhurt. As we said goodbye to one another at the end of the evening, little

---

[35] John 15:5 (MSG).

did I know that his story was about to become intertwined with mine.

During the next day at work, whilst having some personal space in a quiet counselling room, the Holy Spirit came upon me in great power with this revelation: my counselling job of three and a half years was about to end, and quickly.

This was an exciting encounter with God but also a very scary one. I needed this job for financial security since it provided a regular monthly income. I hadn't found another in all my searching over the year since committing to living on the edge. Still, the Holy Spirit beckoned me on, despite my rising apprehension.

Over the next few days, I pondered the situation. 'It's just taking another risk for God, isn't it? I've done it before.'

I looked back with Him on past testimony for reassurance. Over the last seventeen years I had left accountancy for the strange world of psychiatry, started a family on a seemingly inadequate income, left a permanent job for a temporary one and taken voluntary redundancy with no future work in sight. I concluded from my gaze backwards that each risk, taken with God, had been rewarded with His goodness.

Despite these past triumphs of faith, I was still very anxious. My journal records the process I went through:

'It feels like waiting to parachute from a plane. Dare I jump?'

(I was scared of heights!)

Then suddenly it dawned on me that God was speaking to me through the old man's story.

'Oh, God is asking me to make a similar leap, but in the Spirit.'

This revelation strengthened me, and I continued:

'Actually, it's very safe because He is so faithful. It is all about trusting Him just one step further than before into the unknown, unseen future.'

At times like these, we will encounter three main elements: risk, testimony and trust. It feels like we are taking a *risk* but we're not, because God can be fully *trusted*, and we have evidence of this through past *testimony*. But it still can be extremely difficult to go through.

The more I wrote, the stronger I became, and then finally the example of Jesus shone through:

'Jesus was radical, not a part of the crowd. He lived entirely by faith, loving and listening to His Father. I believe that I am called to do the same.'

At this point I made up my mind. Full of the Spirit and convicted of all that God was saying, I was prepared to jump. My mind looked ahead for the right time frame and understood that the next season would begin in the new year. That would require me to give one month's notice from 30th November. There were just ten days to go!

However, as those days went by, one by one, I could feel the strength of my convictions ebbing away like sand through the narrow passage of an hourglass.

Sitting in my office at home, head in hands, struggling with the thought of resigning the next day, I agonised, 'Can I do this by faith?' Money implications were at the forefront of my mind.

Yet right then God was encouraging me to leap. I felt an excruciating fear in my stomach, whilst at the same time God was appealing to me, 'Do you really believe?'

It was not I wanting to get out of that plane, but His Spirit, urging me on.

I thought, 'Do I trust or not?'

Then God spoke, restoring my spiritual strength, like He was drawing my thoughts into His Spirit: 'As you release the old, you will see a whole new world open up to you which is right on your doorstep, not seen before because the timing was not right. Only faith can open your eyes to see it and achieve the purposes that are in My heart. All you have to do is step out and My anointing will fall upon you so that you are ready and equipped to do My will.'

Awash with God's Spirit, deep in His affection, I was able to see a different view of this leap of faith. As I jumped, Jesus would jump too, though only He would be wearing a parachute and would wrap Himself around me, just like the old man's son had done. We were in it together. My job was just to step out and trust Him for the rest.

> God loves us to trust Him because it places us into the faith dimension where He can do His real work.[36]

This vision profoundly affected me, and I tried to share it with Adrienne but broke down in deep, deep sobs. I had never experienced anything like it before, the Spirit working powerfully within me.

Thankfully, through this extraordinary day Adrienne had also been listening to the Holy Spirit, who convicted her that

---

[36] See Hebrews 11:6.

this whole change, though radical, would be ultimately good for the whole family.

This was the security I needed, and I declared finally, 'I've no more doubts. It's got to be right. I'm going for it!'

As the sun rose the next morning, I awoke from my dreams to suddenly remember the enormity of the day.

'Well, it's now or never!' I thought.

Still high in faith-confidence, I wrote out my resignation letter, simple and to the point, and placed it in an envelope. Later that day I went into college, strode purposefully into the human resources department and handed it in. I had jumped.

Then as quickly as the 'old' had gone, the 'new' arrived. My business friend phoned that evening with a proposition: his company would like me to facilitate a Christian retreat day in January. And they were willing to pay me the princely sum of £700.

I was aghast, but instantly agreed since it was the only work on offer beyond my resignation.

INTO THE FUTURE BY FAITH

By the time the day arrived, I had worked out a theme with God entitled, 'Into the Future, by Faith', focussing on Israel's journey into the Promised Land. All our objectives were neatly met in some way. For the company's staff, it was the renewing of vision; for me there was a clear intertwining with my own journey, exploring the 'new land' of business.

> When God moves us into something completely different, we have to grapple with the new that we haven't experienced before. It is a journey where we learn to expect the unexpected! Think of Jacob who

wrestled with God and received a name change that altered his destiny.[37] This is only achievable by faith in the Spirit, who leads us on. His patient guidance moves us forward so that we can enjoy moments of advance. The facilitator role was one for me. It was a small step towards *my* new identity.

I awoke the next morning wondering where my next pay cheque would come from. Since declaring my desire to 'live on the edge', it had taken two and a half years to get to this point. As promised, God had 'catapulted' me out of the college, and I now continued to pursue the identity that would 'fit me like a glove'. But there was no clear direction from God. He had gone very quiet on me.

I thought He would be doing more, but it felt like I was left to work it out on my own. So Ecclesiastes 9:10 came into play:

'Whatever your hand finds to do, do it with all your might.'

Taking on board some advice from my business friend, I set about gaining self-employed status. Before long I had accrued a business bank advisor, an accountant and become a member of The Federation of Small Businesses. I was a small business! Having this identity felt wonderful; now I just had to go and get some work.

With all this abundance of time, I found myself spending hours at home thinking and praying about all sorts of ways to generate finance. I revisited my work identity as a 'Relational Trainer', reasoning that I could fit into what the business world calls 'soft skills'. Then I created material with attractive course

---

[37] See Genesis 32:24-28.

titles that I felt were within my remit, such as stress management, teambuilding and customer care.

But one day I stopped dead in my tracks!

I realised that I had been trying hard to fit my identity into the business world and now remembered that God had specifically called me to bring His presence, not join the world's system.

'How illogical a man can be,' I mused, 'called to go down one road, yet takes another! What took me off? Was it me, the enemy or both?'

As usual I processed this conundrum in my journal, relating to Jesus' life on earth:

'What set Jesus apart in His day was this: He had conviction and authority to be Himself, nothing more, nothing less. He pleased His Father only by continually obeying Him.[38]'

I now realised that I had disobeyed God by forgetting His word to me. So, I repented and made a fresh commitment, declaring, 'Father, I will obey You and please You only.'

I was on a very steep learning curve. In the absence of understanding we tend to go back to what we know. But repentance brings mind renewal in time.[39]

One day God said to me, 'Faith-walking is not for the faint-hearted, but I have put power in you by My Spirit that you will not fail. Keep going out in that power, then you shall see and become who you really are.' And He gave me this warning: 'Do

---

[38] See John 8:28-29.
[39] See Romans 12:1-2.

not compare yourself with others; this always leads to either pride or inadequacy. You're either better or worse than everybody else. Being like this, your faith will go up and down like a yo-yo!'

Soon, God's words proved to be true. Still desperate to find an identity fit, I attended a business showcase at a city hotel to see how trainers compared with my own skillset. This included a Customer Care specialist, who turned out to be someone I could never emulate in a hundred years! I returned home crestfallen, my search for an identity unresolved.

> The astonishing truth is that our loving Father has created all of us to be unique and like no-one else at any time in history. It's a precious identity to find and hold on to. God deeply focussed me on this issue for some time, deliberately emphasising its importance, and here I share it with you. He doesn't want us to make the same mistake as the Israelites, who felt small like grass-hoppers when they saw the giants in the Promised Land, and were punished for their disobedience. This is not the way to inherit or influence any area of life.[40] Here's the lesson for us all to grasp: comparison is the thief of identity.

I attended several Christian business conferences to see if my new identity might be clarified. But no-one understood the meaning of my 'take the message' calling. This left me feeling isolated and confused on this journey of discovery.

But then God gave me a curious piece of the puzzle.

---

[40] See Numbers 13 & 14.

Early one morning, alone with Him, I suddenly found myself in a deep trance[41], a state that I'd never experienced before.

It was like watching a film. Before me unfolded the story of three men at work. For purposes of clarity, I shall refer to them as Tom, Dick and Harry.

Firstly, I saw a large shed where furniture was being made. A man called Tom then walked into the reception area and told one of the workers, Dick, that he had been sent there to work. Dick looked at him and noticed that all he had in his hands were a hammer and a chisel.

'Are you sure you're in the right place?' Dick asked.

'Yes,' said Tom. 'This is where I've been sent.'

Dick couldn't see how Tom would help them to make furniture with only these tools. He was perplexed.

'Well,' Dick said, 'you'd better sit over there until we can think of a job to give you.'

Tom waited patiently.

Presently another man, Harry, appeared and introduced himself. He was the manager. Upon hearing Tom's story, he too was perplexed.

'Have you got a worksheet on you?' he asked.

Tom produced the sheet from his top pocket and, sure enough, he was in the right place.

Harry sat next to him and pondered the situation.

'Tell me, who was it that sent you?'

'The Good Boss,' said Tom.

---

[41] A trance is a visual state in which revelation is received. For a biblical example, see Peter's vision in Acts 10:9-23.

'Ah!' A flicker of understanding crossed Harry's face. 'The Good Boss sent me here too. Well, I'm sure He knows what He's doing. So why don't you just sit here, and some work will turn up for you in due course.'

Later that day, Harry noticed that Tom was no longer sitting there, and as he gazed out of the window, he spotted him busy at work on the outside of another shed next door. Harry pursued his curiosity and discovered to his surprise that Tom's line of work was not making furniture at all but restoring dilapidated sheds. So he invited Tom back, for there was much work for him to do.

This vision left me profoundly stirred yet still mystified. All I tentatively gleaned was that I was Tom, my business friend was Harry and training work was symbolised by furniture-making. I had a set of tools, but what did the job of 'restoring dilapidated sheds' mean? At least it was something to hold on to as hope for future work.

I now entered a time of immense struggle. Over the next few months my emotions were often in turmoil, with sleepless nights, as I grappled with the aftermath of the vision. I just didn't know what I was supposed to be doing, whilst close friends and family looked on in a sort of sympathetic confusion.

At one time, God pointed out that my struggle was similar to a butterfly emerging from its chrysalis sac; my exertion in this season would eventually lead to full development and 'flight'.

It became clear that for this process to work, I had to go through it with Him only, learning that He was more than sufficient. And He intimated, 'It's just Me and you, you and Me.'

This reinforced my '23 Aug Promise'. When God gives us a profound mystery from the depths of the Spirit,[42] it's only by His Spirit that we may proceed. We might look in many different places for a way forward, but there is only one way: through a close relationship with God.

Then one day the dawning of hope arrived through events that unfolded in quick succession, starting with Father God directly answering my persistent question, 'What is the message of Christ to business?'

He said, 'There is only one message: everything that anyone needs is to be found in Christ. It is not in people, systems or brands. Your leap of faith, jumping from the airplane, was in Christ and that's where you must stay in order to see what I have for you.'

These powerful words strengthened my 'in Christ' alignment. I began to feel a total release from the training work identity that I had created, and excitedly began to share my awakening with others, in short stages as the revelation unfolded.

'I'm not a Training Consultant at all!' I informed my business friend, now Managing Director of the company. 'It's something far more spiritual, more overtly Christian.'

I couldn't say any more because that's all I had. But he graciously accepted my blundering that day.

A short time later the revelation translated into an actual job, to be performed at the training company. Full of the Spirit and alone in the boardroom together, I passionately shared God's idea with my friend: to employ me as a Business

---

[42] Referred to by Paul in 1 Corinthians 2:10.

Chaplain. He sat quietly and prayed, whilst I enjoyed the moment with ecstatic confidence.

I'd been here before with this business when God had said, 'Go to the interview as if the job is already yours.' Dumbfounded at being unsuccessful, God had reassured me by paradoxically saying, 'The job is still yours.' And here I was, with God's job that fitted with my new identity. I didn't need to wait for the confirmation, which came a few days later, to know that. On my way home I was bursting with elation and thankfulness. It's a day I'll never forget; such was the relief of finding the next piece of the puzzle. It had taken a year since resigning from the college. Now I was about to re-enter paid employment. I had a spring in my step.

> As we persist through the strangeness of divine mystery, be assured that God's faithfulness will at some point translate into recognisable fruit. As Jesus promised, 'Ask and it will be given to you; seek and you will find; knock and the door will be opened to you. For everyone who asks receives; the one who seeks finds; and to the one who knocks, the door will be opened.'[43]

However, my job was almost stolen before it started. I attended a business breakfast in a majestic setting amongst parkland and a lake in a neighbouring town. High in confidence, I networked liberally with numerous strangers over tasty bacon and Brie stuffed rolls.

I expressed my new job title, 'Business Chaplain', with enthusiasm when sharing my work credentials, but became less sure of myself when I met with opposition. Some were quite

---

[43] Matthew 7:7-8.

subtle, offered with a wry smile, whilst others scathingly demeaned my terminology. For them 'Business Chaplain' was too religious. Some had indeed been churchgoers in the past but had moved on to what they considered to be superior forms of belief.

I came away troubled by the conflict, glad to escape my humiliation. Yet my immediate thought was, 'Oh dear, I'd better change my business vocabulary.'

I got home and, in desperation to conform, began rethinking my work identity. But after an hour or so something didn't feel right. My disquiet led me to stop what I was doing and instead re-read what God had said to me recently in my journal. As I reconnected with my 'in Christ' distinction, I became convicted that I had reverted to worldly ways, forgetting who I was whilst people-pleasing instead of God-pleasing.

> We need Holy Spirit wisdom and discernment to understand how fragile a new 'in Christ' identity is in the early months; and to be aware that we have an enemy intent on stealing it.[44]

Later, God sought to strengthen this 'position' with a fresh word, saying, 'Take heart and keep your eyes on Me. Do not forget or this world will consume you; then you will be fit for nothing. There is much work to be done. I have not put a faint heart in you, but one of power, love and a sound mind.'[45]

Consequently, I wrote down a focussed description of what being a Business Chaplain would entail:

---

[44] See John 10:10.
[45] cp. 2 Timothy 1:7 (NKJV).

'I will fulfil my job by providing spiritual support to company personnel whilst praying and interceding for the business.'

Then I made my first visit to the team. Fifty miles southwest of my hometown were thirty people waiting to see what their new Business Chaplain looked like. I arrived at my destination in a quiet village setting with time to spare, drove into a car park space and entered a plush office environment. They were a mixed bunch of very amiable people and listened with patient attention to my laptop presentation. Though I spelled out my credentials, such as pastoral support and prayer, a few still couldn't understand why I was there. I felt a slight unease but pressed on, since this feeling was by now a common one. They hadn't known what to do with me before and clearly some still felt that way!

One such person asked me, 'What does God have to do with corporate training?'

'Good question!' I thought.

I paused, unsure, but then the Holy Spirit helped, and I replied with something that surprised even me: 'Imagine God as a satellite in the sky, able to connect two parties on earth. It would make marketing a lot easier if you asked Him for clients.'

He didn't say a lot after that!

> If you're ever stuck for what to say, remember Jesus' instruction, 'The Holy Spirit will give you the right words when the time comes.'[46]

In the ensuing weeks it became clear who was responding to my services. I set up regular appointments for support with

---

[46] Luke 12:12 (MSG).

prayer on work matters. Involving God together, we met at all sorts of times of the day, whenever and wherever it suited them. At other times I met with the company trustees as 'intercessor'. So I continued the art of working flexibly that God had introduced me to earlier in my career.

These responsibilities were a source of great joy and satisfaction because I was at last beginning to outwork my calling by literally 'taking the message of Christ to the business community', from my 'in Christ' identity. His presence was the key that opened the door for the message to be released, in the form of Word (the Bible) and Spirit (prophetic word) as and when the need arose, and I loved supporting the people together with Him. Yet somehow, I still couldn't settle back entirely, because the Holy Spirit continued to stir me so that I ached for more. And I wondered what it could possibly be!

One Sunday an itinerant minister from California came to our church. His visit was to set in motion a series of events that accelerated my ministry in ways I could never have imagined, as is promised to us in Ephesians 3:20.

I approached him after his sermon to describe my 'job from heaven'. Then, knowing him to be a well-travelled man, I asked, 'Do you happen to know anyone else in the world that has a similar calling?'

To my astonishment he did, describing a man back in California who was called to something very similar, but in finance as a Venture Capitalist. He went further, assuring me that on his return home he would mention our chat to his friend. I supplied my name and address.

I must confess that in all my ups and downs of recent years, I doubted that I would ever hear anything, but he was true to his word. A month later a large package arrived through the post addressed to me. It was quite heavy, and I wondered what on earth it could be. I ripped it open impatiently, to find inside three books and a letter inviting me to a conference in late October, hosted by Nehemiah Partners in Los Angeles.

'They are a collection of people called to transform the marketplace. If you can find the flight money, I will pay your conference fees and you can stay with me.' So wrote the Venture Capitalist.

A quick inspection of these books revealed something that gripped my immediate attention. They described how God was raising up faith pioneers with the task of impacting the world of business. I just knew that I was one of them! In excitement I told Adrienne and read the letter to her.

I was convicted to go but hesitated. Not being a seasoned globetrotter, I didn't relish the prospect of going halfway around the world on my own! I needed someone to accompany me and reasoned out loud, 'This person would have to be a close friend who knows me well and understands my calling.'

Then I suddenly realised who it should be. 'It's you, Adrienne!' I exclaimed.

She loved the idea, but then we both had concerns about our three young daughters. We couldn't just leave them on their own whilst we jetted off to the USA. There was no precedent for that in our family life. But God's miracle timing came into play, which helped reinforce our decision. Unexpectedly, the girls asked if they could go away for a weekend with the church youth group sailing a canal barge. It just happened to be the very same time as the LA conference! When we agreed, they were delighted to go on such an adventure whilst we went on ours. So that took care of that. But what about the cost? Thanks to the kindness of our host, only the airfare would be needed.

On looking at my bank statement, I found, not surprisingly, that I had the exact amount with five pounds to spare. God was definitely in this!

We booked the flights on Tuesday morning of 11th September 2001, unaware of what was about to happen in New York City later that day when the Twin Towers would be destroyed by terrorist planes. When we saw the live, horrific TV footage that afternoon, fear tried to get a grip on us, and we thought of cancelling because of the threat of further attacks. But when we asked God if we should proceed with the plan, He replied, 'Am I not greater than any terrorist?'

I took this for a yes and we did proceed, by faith.

> There are times when God's people are caught up in the high drama of world events. Acting by faith centres us on God and not on those circumstances, however risky and scary they may appear to us.

In the wake of the terrorist attacks security was tight, and as we boarded our flight in Amsterdam, we were to experience one of God's most amazing divine appointments in our whole life. As we sat waiting for take-off, the pilot proceeded to introduce himself and the cabin crew in the usual fashion. But then he continued with an unusual announcement:

'I want to tell you about someone who lived five thousand years ago. He was a man of God called Nehemiah who was strong and determined, unafraid of opposition whilst achieving great things. Let us be like him; so that if anyone aboard this flight tries to threaten us with a bomb, do not be afraid, but together we can defeat his objective by overcoming him with all necessary force. Because God is greater than any terrorist!'

Then, as if we were all in a church meeting, he added, 'Since we are going to be with each other for some considerable time, why not introduce yourself to your neighbour. May I wish you all a pleasant flight.'

This experience was indeed just like being at church and we chatted with delight to our fellow passengers. But of course, his reference to Nehemiah was quite astonishing since we were going to a Nehemiah Partners' conference!

This confirmed not only that we were right in our decision to go, but also that we would be perfectly safe, at the heart of God's purposes.

Our host was waiting for us at LAX airport with a warm welcome, and as he drove us the twenty miles to his home, chatting amiably, we felt humbled by the spacious land and the reason we had come. This feeling then turned to amazement as he drove us into a gated community and to a large family home with its own private pool. We were beginning to feel generously looked after so far from home.

God was also affirming my ministry. On the first morning of the two-day conference at a local church, we met the organiser who, by way of introduction, looked at me with a broad grin and said, 'I know you've got it. I can see it in your eyes!' In other words, we both had the same pioneer calling to the business world. I felt the strong undergirding of vindication, for after two years of loneliness and misunderstanding amongst God's people, I had at last found a similar heart.

As proceedings began, I was able to encourage the slender number of participants with our testimony about how God had affirmed the conference through the pilot at Amsterdam. People were astounded. But much more was to follow as God set about powerfully inspiring us through a highly prophetic time in the main sessions and during social interaction with each other.

Much of the teaching confirmed what God had already deposited in me over recent years relevant to God at work. Then there was a significant prophetic insight, new to me: the notion of 'kings' and 'priests' in the workplace, heavenly titles given for its transformation as aligned to God's kingdom culture.

> Within each born-again believer is the DNA of Christ which carries His identity of prophet, priest and king. Here the priest is manifest in the 'helper' and king in the 'worker'.[47]

This insight carried enormous significance for me. At last it began to make sense that this priestly role was the job identity God said would 'fit me like a glove'.

The next day was Sunday and along came an opportunity to try out my priestly identity when we attended my host's church. At the end of the service, we ministered to businesspeople with a power that surprised both them and us. Affirmed in their own calling, they were deeply touched by God's presence to the point of tearful elation.

Then on our final morning, God spoke a word into my future. As we gathered closely together in the kitchen of our host's beautiful home, holding hands in prayer, someone with a word of knowledge said, 'Within six weeks of returning to the UK you will have work.'

Back at LAX airport for the flight home we were to receive yet more amazing favour when we were upgraded to business

---

[47] See 1 Peter 2:5,9; Revelation 1:6.

class. There we were in our large blue armchairs, drinking tea from china cups, savouring the kingdom promotion that God had clearly given us. We were ablaze in the Holy Spirit the whole journey home, like two rockets that had been blasted into a new orbit.

Once home in the UK, and exhausted from jet lag, I realised that I had booked myself into something else the following weekend. I wondered whether to go, but its subject matter reinvigorated me. It was called 'Spirituality in the Workplace'!

Throughout this conference I continued to blaze away in my fresh orbit, and this fire burnt into numerous conversations. I just couldn't help it! Chief amongst my contributions was my recent revelation about Christ's 'kings' at work. I was in my element, speaking into these workers' lives in my priestly role. It felt amazing!

Then something astonishing happened. During one of the breaks a fellow delegate approached me, interested in my use of the word 'king'. He was an entrepreneur and as we chatted together, he explained his curiosity. Recently he had received a prophetic word in church declaring that he would become a 'king' in the workplace.

So, there we were. God had miraculously brought together a priest and a king – two men, the first to whom God had said 'you will have work within six weeks of arriving back in the UK'; the other carrying a 'kingly' mantle and looking for someone to affirm it. We were a perfect match, and my kingdom ministry was truly launched a short time later when we started work together, the first of many 'Work with God' partnerships.

I had at last found my kingdom identity at work, and it was a delight to me, found only in Christ. As a son/daughter of Father God, yours is waiting there for you too. Follow the keys on the next page, enjoy the adventure that awaits and expect the unexpected.

KEYS

The three stages to a kingdom identity:

1. Hunger for more of God.

2. Seek Him out of love, not need.

3. Work with Him as the Holy Spirit leads.

PRAYER

Father God,
I love You with all my heart, mind, soul and strength.
Thank you that You have a kingdom identity waiting for me.
I give You my life afresh, so take me as I am and lead me into
all You have for me in the sphere of work.
Amen.

CHAPTER SEVEN

The Other 'God'

Unveiling and Defeating a Hidden Foe

'Jesus said, "How could you worship two gods at the same time? You will have to hate one and love the other or be devoted to one and despise the other. You can't worship the true God while enslaved to the god of money."'

Matthew 6:24 (TPT)

If you are serious about developing a heavenly identity where you work, you will have to sooner or later win a spiritual battle over 'Master Money'. Why? Because this personification of a real seductive power is your number one competitor for whose kingdom you are truly serving.

Here I describe my spiritual journey from paid work in the world system to 'presence work' in heaven, with keys for others to find.

Before I became a Christian, money was everything. I was raised in a middle-class family and lacked for nothing. Money was what enabled this material lifestyle, though I wouldn't have called myself a 'worshipper' of it; only that my life was dependent on it. The more I could have, the happier I would be. It was my hope for a better life, and everyone I knew, family and friends, were the same. It was the accepted way to be. We all enjoyed the thrill it gave, the power of purchase. And we all wanted more, unaware of being unwittingly seduced.[48]

When I gave my life to Christ at twenty-seven, along with my wife Adrienne, this mode of thinking started to change for us both. Money steadily began to descend the priority list as our trust in God increased. This led to some surprising decisions.

During our early married years, we didn't think we could afford to raise a family but went ahead after speaking to faith-filled church friends who said they wouldn't hesitate. When our first child was born, Adrienne became a full-time mum, giving up her banking career, consequently losing a cheap mortgage and high salary. This choice didn't make any economic sense to the way we'd lived before. Neither did a career change for me around the same time, when I switched to a different job that suited me much better but paid a lot less. Yet God led us to trust Him.

This wasn't an easy or quick journey of faith. We went along with God as much as we dared, whilst secretly clinging to some fall-back positions due to lack of trust in Him. Just in case things didn't work out, we could always move to a cheaper house and sell the car. But as events transpired, neither became necessary because God gently led us along the path of faith through various means such as receiving gifts of food and money that arrived at just the right time. This way of life was underpinned by the biblical principle of tithes and offerings.[49]

---

[48] See Ephesians 2:2 (TPT).
[49] See Malachi 3:8-12.

It didn't always look affordable to tithe in a month when the water bill was the same amount, but we trusted God's word and over time saw how He orchestrated our financial life of flowing in and out at just the precise moment. Miraculously, within three years we had moved to an even larger home to accommodate ourselves and now three children.

> Trusting God on a journey of faith, whatever our economic circumstances, is the first step to overcoming our reliance on the 'other god'. It's very challenging because this way of life contradicts much of what we've been taught in the world. But God is a faithful Father who will see us safe and blessed if we choose to trust Him.

Some years later, God went about changing my mindset towards money through a journey of steps, each one more radical than the last.

The first step came when I was a full-time college lecturer and my department staffing budget was cut, resulting in several of us having to reapply for a limited number of jobs now available. I didn't get one. Instead, I was given various options on the way forward, one of which was a small voluntary redundancy package. I wouldn't have chosen this and agonised over what to do for many days. But God clearly indicated this choice when I spoke to my pastor about it. This left me very apprehensive. I'd always had full-time work and there were large monthly bills to pay.

> We won't realise that money is our first security and not God until we arrive at this sort of juncture in our lives. But it's an important moment to reach, for Master

> Money, our hidden foe, is now unmasked as we choose
> God as the only One to fully trust.

God didn't let me down. He provided a variety of training work from my previous department at the college, on top of which He added the half-time post of college counsellor.

A couple of years later, the second step arrived when I was bored with my Christian life and told God of my desire to spiritually 'live on the edge'. This entailed a greater trust in Him on a journey of faith.

God took me at my word, and one consequence of this was a gracious promise that has established me upon His provision ever since. Waiting on Him one morning, He said, 'No matter how long it takes or how many mistakes you make, I will supply your needs. So do not look to money but to Me, for in Me is everything you need.'

> When we step out to have more of God, we encounter a
> steep learning curve; but He is utterly faithful to our
> progress when our close relationship is at the heart of it.

Sometime later God told me that my counselling job was soon to end because of the 'Work with God' ministry He had recently birthed in me. The challenge to Master Money now increased significantly, while I struggled to fully believe God's assurance of provision. Once again I came face to face with my real security: a regular monthly income. With no imminent job on the horizon, fear quickly replaced faith.

As I agonised over this situation, the Holy Spirit beckoned me on, encouraging me to look back at God's faithfulness to us over the years. In so many situations Master Money had not been allowed to dominate our big decisions such as family and career choices.

He also reassured me by promising that as I let go of the 'old' (my job), the new would come. Sure enough, after resigning I received a surprise invitation to facilitate a Christian retreat day, paying more than I'd been earning in a month! Once again God had supplied me with paid work His way, and it was a great success.

It would have given me a natural sense of security had this wonderful provision been a formula for future work, but it wasn't in God's plan. The Spirit now led me away from this old thinking and Master Money's influence, into a season in which I received no paid work for fourteen months!

> Not everyone is invited to go to a place of faith like this one. But if we are, it is a hard and challenging journey to embrace because the culture we've lived by all our lives has now been quashed. The means of exchange has become faith, not money. As such, Master Money is rendered powerless. God is now the number One, to trust like never before. For those who choose to enter and are rewarded with this faith realm of the miraculous, here's a question we all face: can I now look to God to be Lord over everything?

Looking back, I call this a season of 'abandonment' because my life was given over exclusively to God. I was completely on my own, without any supportive work colleagues, and at the beginning felt a curious mixture of feelings: freedom and fear; freedom because I had no one to report to and fear because I had no one to report to!

A satisfying thought occurred to me: 'I can do anything I want in work time.' But soon the exhilaration gave way to an anxious thought: 'How am I going to survive? I must have paid work!'

> In this place of loneliness (except for the presence of God) the work at hand is to develop a healthy balance between these two elements – freedom and fear – to the point that it becomes the norm for our lives. The rewarding consequence is this: we will become completely free to work according to God's designs whilst being transformed from fear of financial lack into a holy fear, born out of our love for God and a desire to put Him first in everything. As Jesus directed, 'Seek first his kingdom and his righteousness, and all these things will be given to you as well.'[50]

Still, the hardest challenge remained: being devoid of paid work; no purpose, no fulfilment, wasted, unsatisfying. And I was only two months into the process!

I knew I had been obedient to God, but it was like He was not enough. Faith was not enough. I was starting a business ministry, but what was its nature? Whom was it for and how was I to get paid?

I spent a day with my pastor trying to explain this predicament. We sat in his car amid picturesque countryside when I burst into tears, unable to control the anguish within. 'I just don't understand what's going on!' He couldn't give me any easy answers, but his concern and prayers were enough to stem the downward flow of despair.

---

[50] Matthew 6:33.

I had not been like this before when I had had guaranteed, paid work. God had pulled away everything except Himself, and it revealed a lack of faith in such a short time. I doubted God and I never thought I would do that, particularly after all the numerous times He had encouraged me in the past.

So I humbled myself in prayer: 'I repent of doubting You, Lord. I know You are utterly faithful.'

> As God works to strip away the worldliness which so easily clings to us, our true hearts are revealed! Through repentance, He puts us back together again, now aligned to the image and mind of Christ.[51]

Several months into this journey and still struggling without paid work, Father God revealed the faith-position where He wanted me to be.

He said, 'You ask, "Where is the work? Where is the pay?" I say, "What is that to you?" Your priorities are wrong. Seek first the kingdom. Do not jump ship or make decisions in desperation, in frustration, in anger or in despair, for you are not *in* any of these. My *bullseye* for you is that you are in Me, in Christ. Have I not supplied you with sufficiency more lavish than any working man? Tell me, when have you been in need? Tell Me, when was the last time you were begging on the streets, or crying out to be saved?'

And Father was right! He had provided miraculously for us, such as gifts and a small part time job for my wife.

---

[51] See Romans 12:1-2.

Sometimes God speaks uncomfortable truths to us, like He did to Job.[52] But as we acknowledge that He is right, we will shift into a new faith-position where we discover hidden revelation. Mine was a 'heavenly' identity that says, 'I'm secure because I am in Christ,' and everything I need is to be found there. I had shifted away from an 'earthbound' identity that said, 'I'm secure because I have an income.'

Once I had embraced this revelation, my work prospects started to dramatically change. I had been on the fringe of a corporate training company for two years, looking for some type of paid work. But now God made it clear to me that I was to be their Business Chaplain, and miraculously this Christian company agreed!

The only problem was they offered me a part-time job on a small salary for just a six-month pilot project. I complained to God that it wasn't a full-time wage, but He just replied, 'This is it for now.' Clearly, we had very different expectations!

Sometimes our expectations run ahead of what God is doing and we must deal with disappointment. This happens because our earthbound identities are so deeply engrained. How we long for the known worldly practices and are so slow to embrace unknown heavenly ones, even when our Father is encouraging us on with His perfect love and patience! He always leads us towards the best He has waiting for us to embrace.

---

52 See Job 38.

I had to face the choice God was giving me, so I accepted the job, and after the first enjoyable month it was a huge relief to eventually receive a pay cheque – precious indeed after a fourteen-month wait!

Over time, the 'in Christ' identity became the security in my life whilst the full-time salary never did materialise. Instead, God remained on track to lessen the power of Master Money and take me into even greater dependence upon Him. We now moved on to step three.

The chaplaincy season ended with a smooth transition into my own 'Work with God' business clients. I formed contracts with these 'partners' (in faith), invoicing them on an hourly rate basis for work done. This consisted of working in God's presence with them, revealing kingdom strategies and blueprints using discernment, prophetic word and intercession.

Then, after five years of steady partnership growth, God directed me to an alternative type of financial arrangement. He said, 'Stop charging. Freely you have received, so freely give. You have no contract with me; have none with them.'

God reminded me of this scripture when Jesus sent out the first disciples:

'Freely you have received the power of the kingdom, so freely release it to others.'[53]

Contracts are earthly and temporal. When the 'in Christ' identity becomes our main security, we are set free from Master Money and are ready for more of heaven's influence over our finances at work. What was not possible before is now, because we have come up

---

[53] Matthew 10:8 (TPT).

eternally higher and experienced a greater fullness of Christ.

The idea of not charging seemed crazy for a moment. But I quickly discerned it was of God, being used to His outrageous ways by now! I was excited by the prospect of becoming 'gift-based' and informed my partners straight away. Then, as I thought about the implications, I wondered how the tax system would view this change.

A few weeks later we found out, when Adrienne and I made an appointment to see our local Tax Status Officer. We told him our situation and he listened patiently but was left flummoxed! He couldn't see how God's idea of 'gift-based' might sit well within the self-employment tax rules. We left his office that morning with a deep sense of hopelessness, unsure of the way forward.

A few days later, however, we did rejoice at one thing, when we received his official memo of our meeting through the post. He gave a surprisingly accurate spiritual description of my 'in Christ' identity: 'Andy Black is not accountable to anyone on earth.'

Still, the task to accommodate God's idea continued to challenge the tax authorities to the hilt and there were many months of indecision like waves of the sea, ebbing and flowing. We were never quite sure just how this dilemma was to be sorted. Then one day breakthrough came by a divine appointment with a senior tax official, who gave me a recognised status at last. It was a great relief to be able to do what God had asked of me with the agreement of the tax establishment.

When the worldly authorities cannot accommodate what God has asked of us, this is a 'clash of kingdoms' moment. Our new heavenly identity must now grapple with an earthbound system! It's in the way of divine progress, so what can we do? Well, God wouldn't ask us to do something if it were not possible to achieve. So as we return to God with our conundrum, He helps us process it, and when breakthrough finally arrives, we exhibit a cry of great relief and carry on with Him and His counter-cultural plans. It's kingdom business on earth!

I came to realise something of profound significance associated with moving from contract to 'gift-based'. It was this: I was now working not directly with partners first, but with God. This meant that the amount of finance was to come from Him, not them. The partners therefore needed to consult God about how much He wanted them to give me, no longer restricted to a pre-agreed contract.

The tax officer had been more accurate than he knew, for I was now under God's authority and freer from Master Money than ever.

Another dimension also came to the fore: that of 'time'. The world lives by the maxim, 'Time is money.' But for me this no longer applied. Payment was no longer geared to the amount of time I worked but according to how much God deemed I should have.

When we work exclusively with God, the financial reward cannot be questioned. Faith alignment replaces work achievement as the priority. Sometimes it's lucrative, other times not, but God knows what we need. And we must be careful not to emotionally manipulate people in this process to extract money from them, however much we may think we deserve it. Godly contentment is the key to this, and in Philippians 4:12-13 Paul reveals its secret.

Step four was revealed to me one day as I sat on a hillside in glorious sunshine and looked across the valley to a farmhouse with its outbuildings and farm machinery. Sheep and cows were in the surrounding fields and a dog was barking. I began to think about the spread of land owned by the farmer. This was his land because he had paid, or was in the process of paying, money for it. My thoughts didn't surprise me since I know how this world works. But God did surprise me when He said, 'Do not be restricted to what money can buy. Look around you and see land and buildings owned by money restrictions. But "the earth is the Lord's, and everything in it."'[54]

Relating to money restricts us, keeping us earth-bound and separate from the kingdom identity that is our true inheritance. God does not want us constrained by anything, but to have freedom in Christ, being seated with Him in heavenly places.[55]

Through these four steps, God had helped me to unveil and win many battles against the seductive power of Master Money. Now, as restrictions lessened again, I was to come into even

---

[54] Psalm 24:1.
[55] See Ephesians 2:6.

more freedom on my journey with Christ into His unlimited kingdom.

KEYS

1. Discern your motives and choose whom you will serve.

2. Determine to win your spiritual battles with Master Money.

3. Follow Jesus into His kingdom.

PRAYER

Lord Jesus,

Thank you that You have overcome the world, that Your kingdom is accessible to all sons and daughters of God.

Help me to love and follow You without limit and be free to enjoy treasures that are beyond what money can buy.

Amen.

The Challenge

Dear reader,

Having now read this book, are you inspired? Have you found Jesus afresh in your working life as you prayed the prayers and applied some keys? As we finish now, I'd like to challenge you further, as I continue to be.

A few years ago, I read about some Christian entrepreneurs who were helping people in other nations to build successful businesses. Their work was providing jobs and developing sustainable communities in some of the poorest places on earth.

'Sounds great!' I thought.

Yet in the next moment, I sensed God give me a different view, saying, 'They are reproducing after their own kind, that is, successful entrepreneurs.' Then He reaffirmed the work He'd commissioned me to do. 'But you are called to build the kingdom, not successful companies; that is, businesses which carry the marks of Christ, the nature of Christ, a reflection of Christ, run by people who have welcomed Me in and are totally sold out for Me and what I represent, including My church, whom I love.'

An overview of the global working community then began to unfold before me when I sensed two distinct business identities, Reproduction and Reflection. The first imitates the world's striving for monetary success, whilst the second demonstrates the genuine image of Christ, founded upon relationship with Him.

I saw further that the Reflection identity is currently very rare and exists in prototype form only. But over time it will fully emerge, whilst the business that compromises with the world will be shaken. Those whose foundation is Christ will stand firm and be a strong tower for their own safety and many others.

As a follower of Jesus (and by that relationship, a citizen of heaven), why would you copy the world's ways with all the hallmarks of your old life when you can pioneer something special together with your Father, prepared for you in your ongoing restoration in Christ?

I believe that you are not so much a product of your past but a prototype of the future – a heavenly future. This means living out aspects of your eternal identity now, pulling the future into your present. As you grow in intimacy with God through your work, you will become more like Christ and better suited to fulfil the original mandate God gave mankind, to reflect Their image on earth.[56]

With this prospect before you and all the heavenly tools needed to get the job done, are you ready to fulfil such a privileged calling upon your life? I hope so, because this is the reason you were 'born again' into such a time as this.

And now, a final prayer:

Father, thank you for calling me to partner with You in my workplace. Help my relationship with You grow deeper in love, so that Your longing can be fulfilled through our togetherness and Your kingdom come as it is in heaven.

In Jesus' name, amen.

---

[56] See Genesis 1:26.

'And as Christ himself is seen for who he really is, who you really are will also be revealed, for you are now one with him in his glory.'

Colossians 3:4 (TPT)

About 'Work with God'

Since its launch in the year 2000, *Work with God* has now partnered in various ways with people in over 100 different job-types in spheres such as education, health and manufacturing.

Through learning to host God's presence privately we have the privilege of seeing Him impact lives publicly: partners growing in Christ to discover such kingdom treasures as the outworking of prophetic words, godly ways of handling finance, clear business vision and other blueprints from heaven. Also called 'kingdom pioneers', it is a joy to see God take them on adventures into the unknown.

In 2016 the ministry enlarged its scope into the literary world. This book is now our third publication.

Further information can be obtained from:

www.workwithgod.co.uk

Other Books by Andy Black

The Helper
ISBN 978-1-911086-03-1

The Helper Workbook
ISBN 978-1-911086-05-5

Work fills our lives for forty hours each week for forty years. It was never intended to be a place where we simply earned our living, but one where we accomplish something of worth. Yet most people don't experience this.

Andy Black embarked upon a career that soon became a journey of torment that lasted for seven long years. Then one day a mysterious voice spoke into his working world, transforming him into someone filled with hope, purpose and confidence.

The accompanying workbook will lead you on a spiritual adventure of enlightenment, uncovering inlaid mysteries about the workplace and helping you to discover fresh hope, purpose and confidence.